Thanks to all who have helped, thanks to the
interaction of materials and intervals.

Artwork By Angus Baird
Page Design By Kristina Pinkert

Published by Idrawalot
PO Box 16744 Seattle WA 98116-0744

Idrawalot books are available through direct distribution
and are also available in a variety of electronic formats.
To contact Idrawalot directly write to addison@idrawalot.com
& angusbaird2@gmail.com

ISBN-13: 978-1468009262

Title: Disillusion of Narrative
Author: Angus Baird
Publisher: Idrawalot
Address: PO Box 16744 Seattle WA 98116-0744
Format: Paperback
Publication Date: January 2012
ISBN-13: 978-1468009262

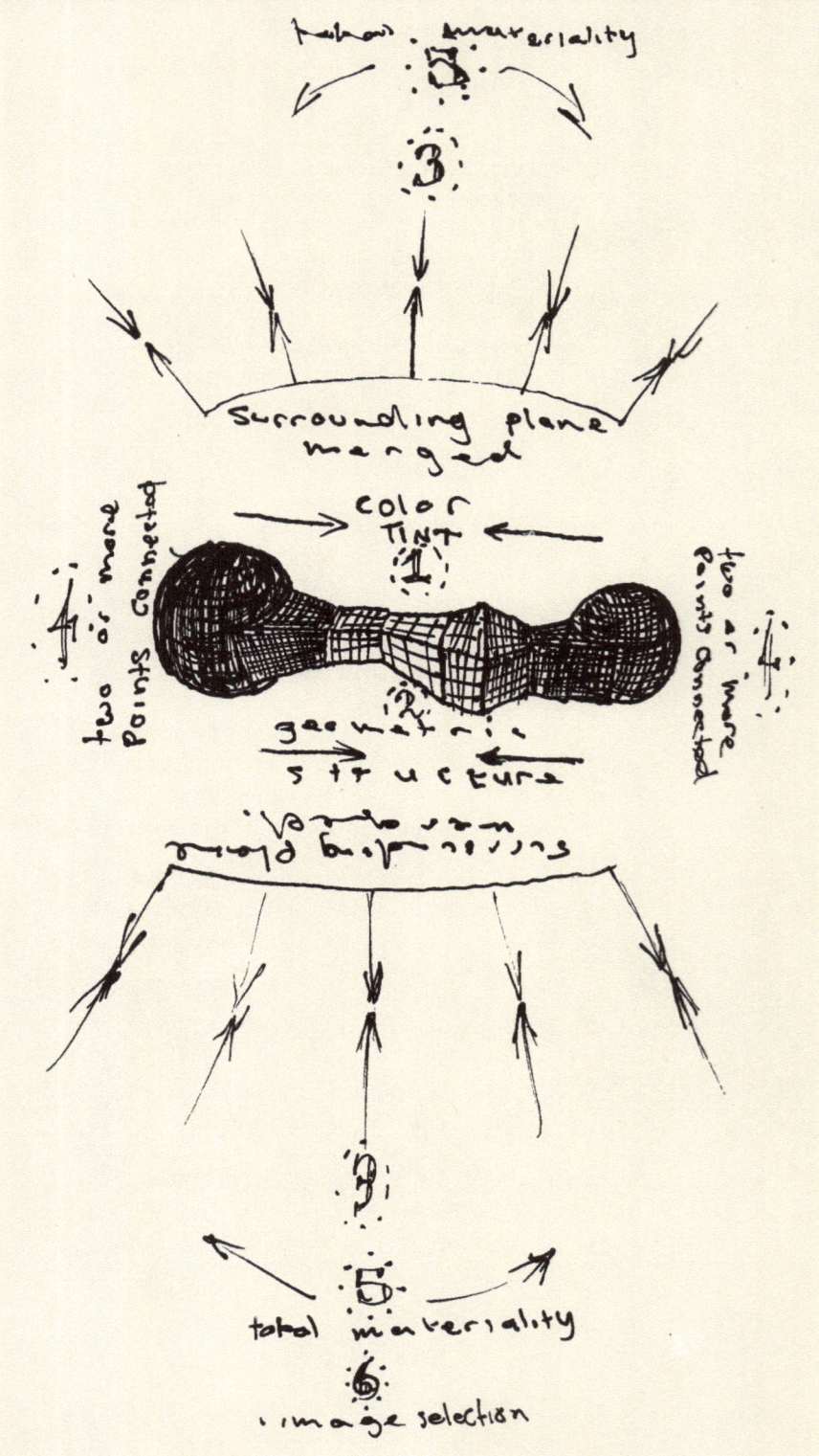

total immateriality

.5.

.3.

Surrounding plane
merged

color
TINT
.1.

two or more points connected

two or more points connected

.2.
geometric
structure

surrounding plane

.3.

.5.
total immateriality

.6.
image selection

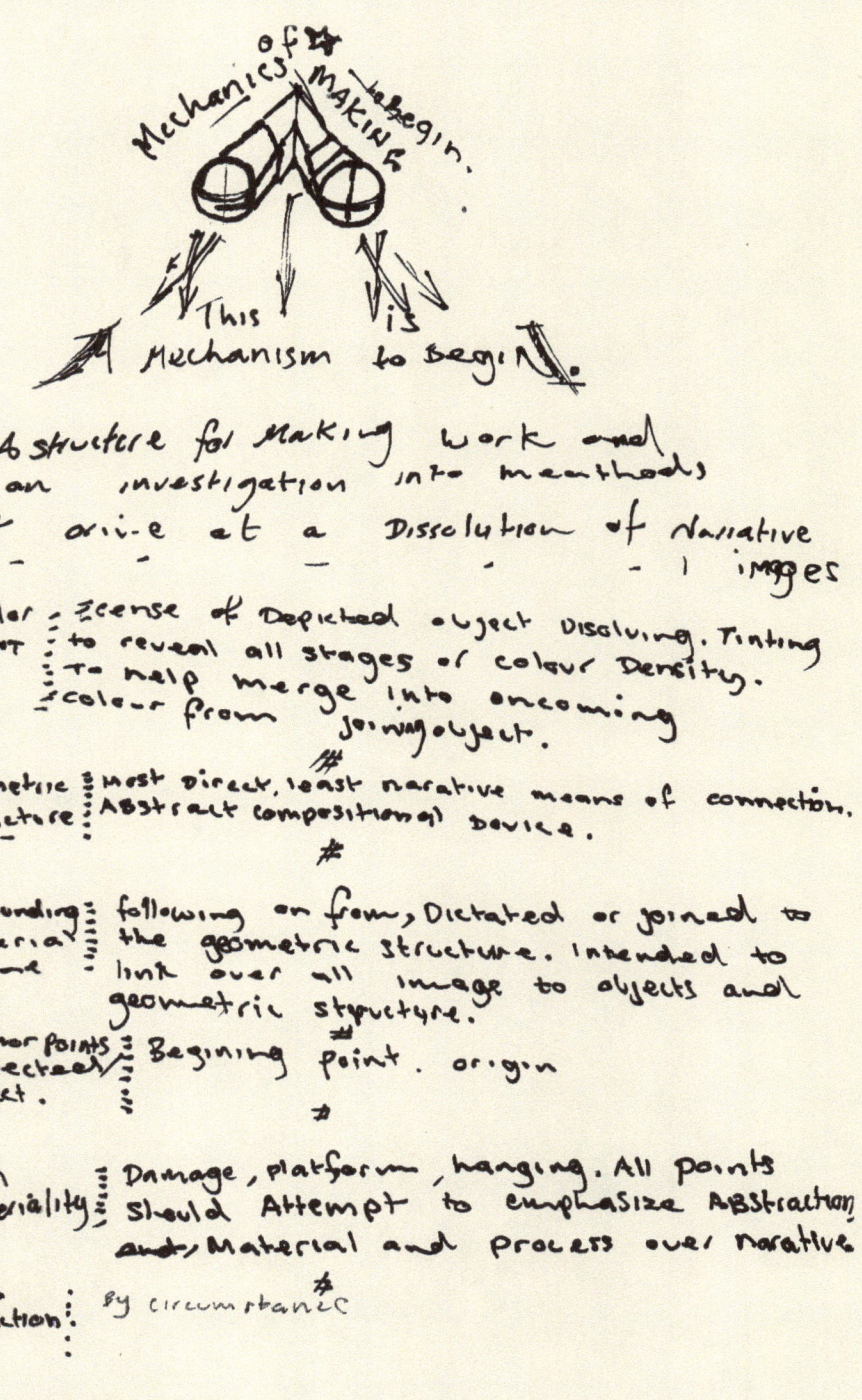

Mechanics of ↗ to begin.
MAKING.

This is Mechanism to begin.

A structure for Making work and
an investigation into meanthods
that arive at a Dissolution of Narrative
in - - - - - - images

1. Color : Eense of Depicted object Disolving. Tinting
   tint : to reveal all stages of colour Density.
        : To help merge into oncoming
        : colour from joining object.

2. geometric : most Direct, least narative means of connection.
   structure : Abstract compositional Device.

3. surrounding : following on from, Dictated or joined to
   Picteria : the geometric structure. Intended to
   Plane : link over all image to objects and
          geometric structure.

4. 2 or mor points : Begining point. origin
   connecteed/ :
   object. :

5. total : Damage, platform, hanging. All points
   materiality : Should Attempt to emphasize Abstraction
              and, Material and process over narative

6. Photo : By circumstance
   selection :

7. Process : mannal.

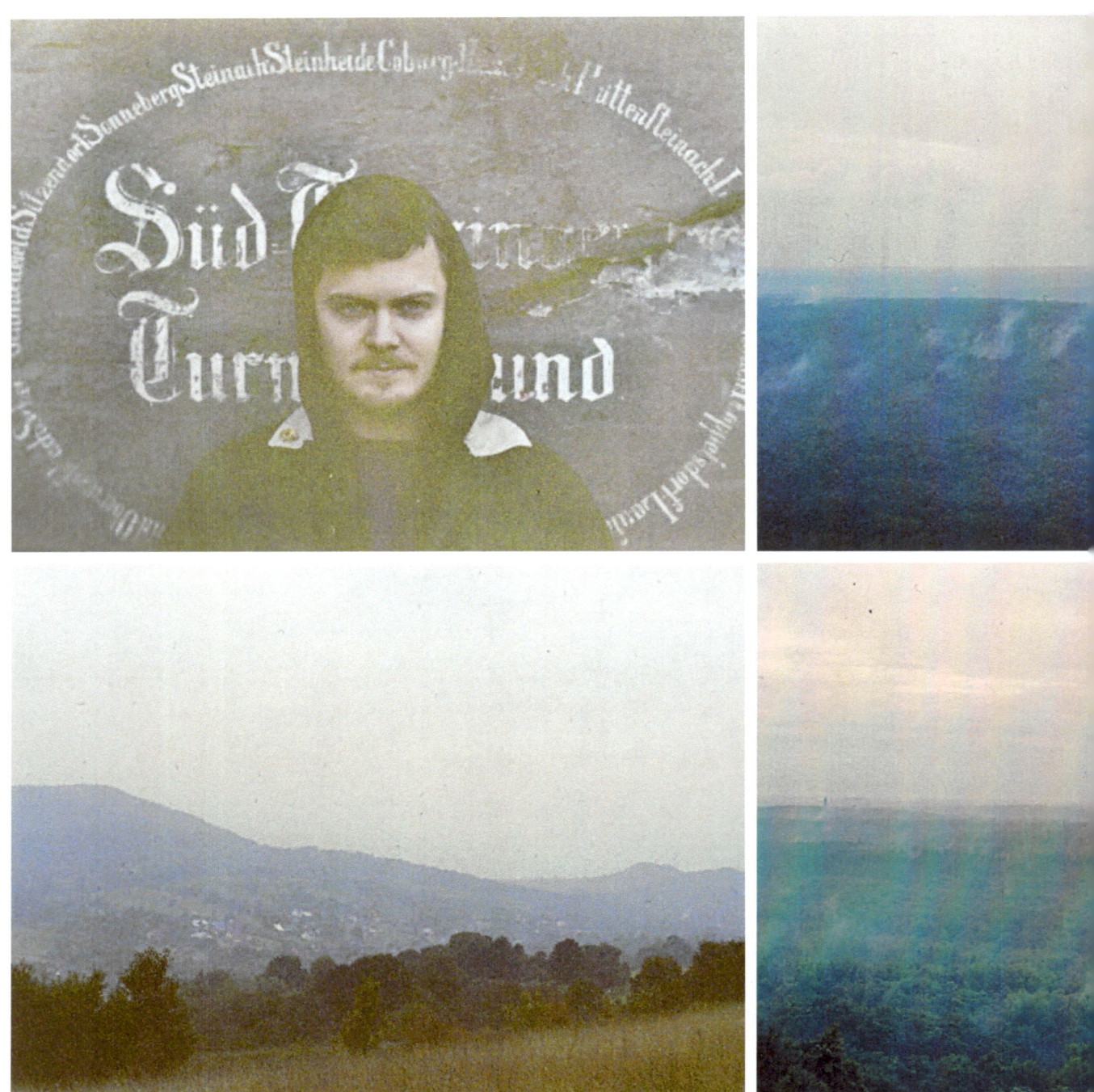

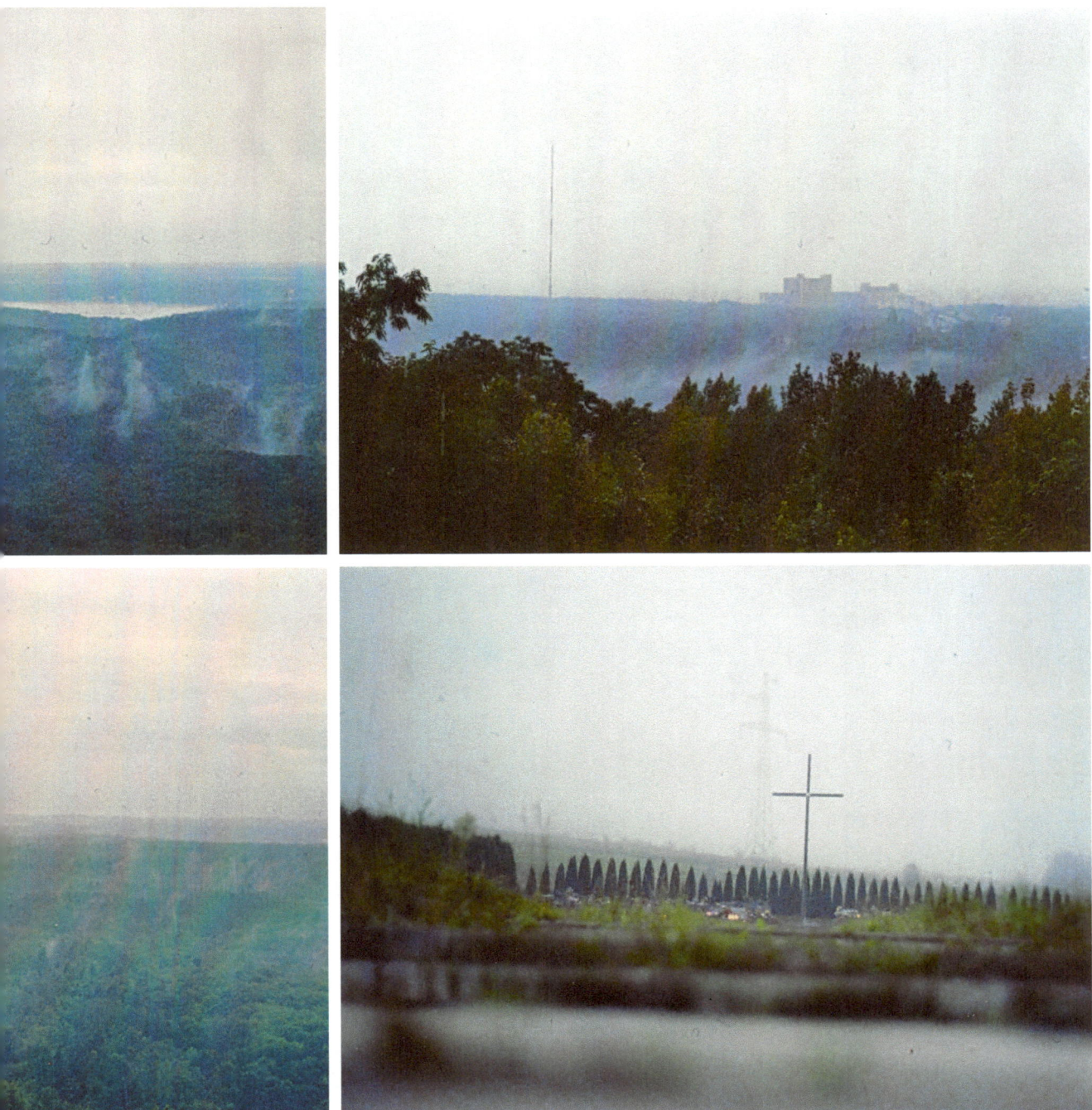

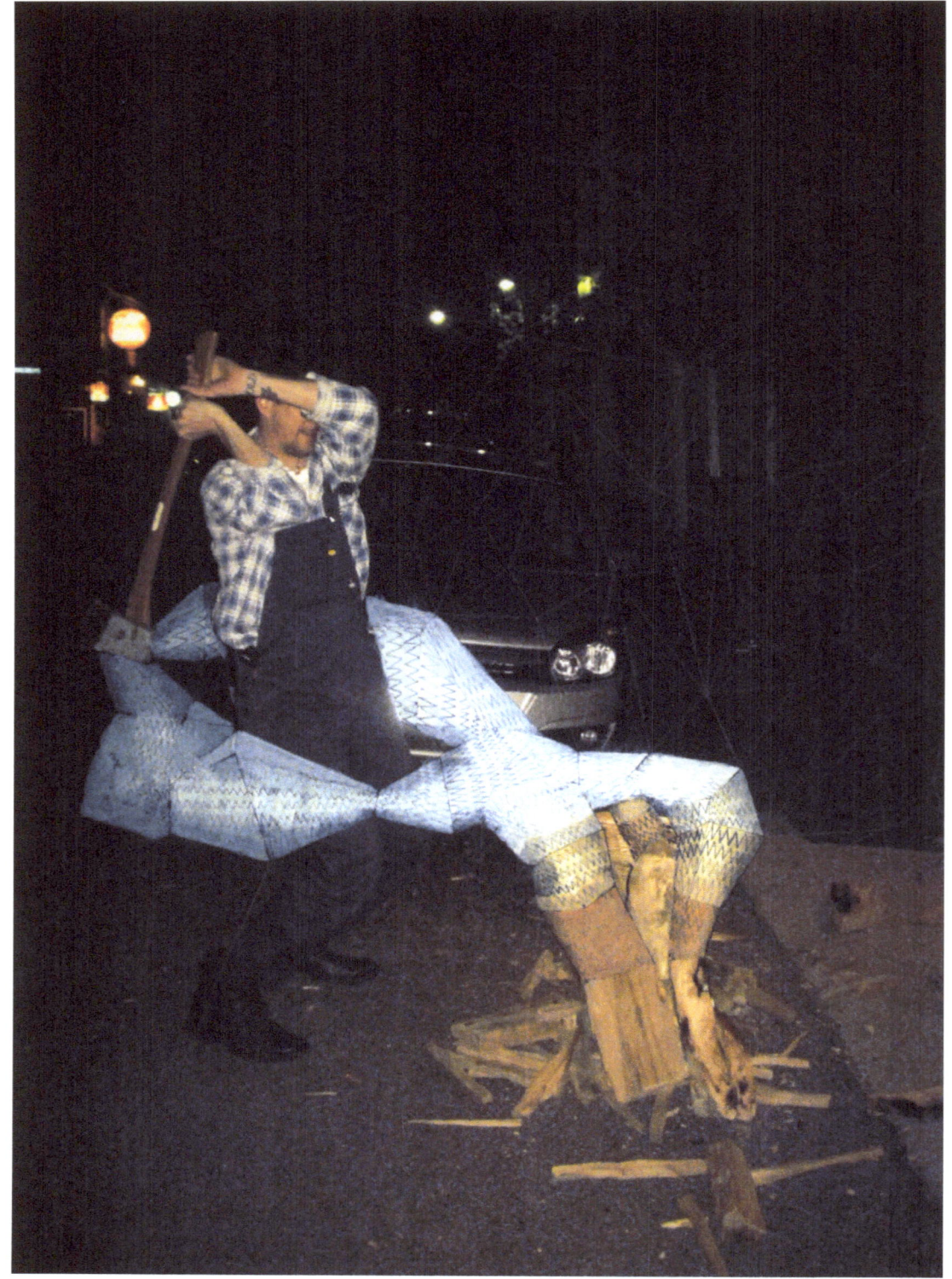

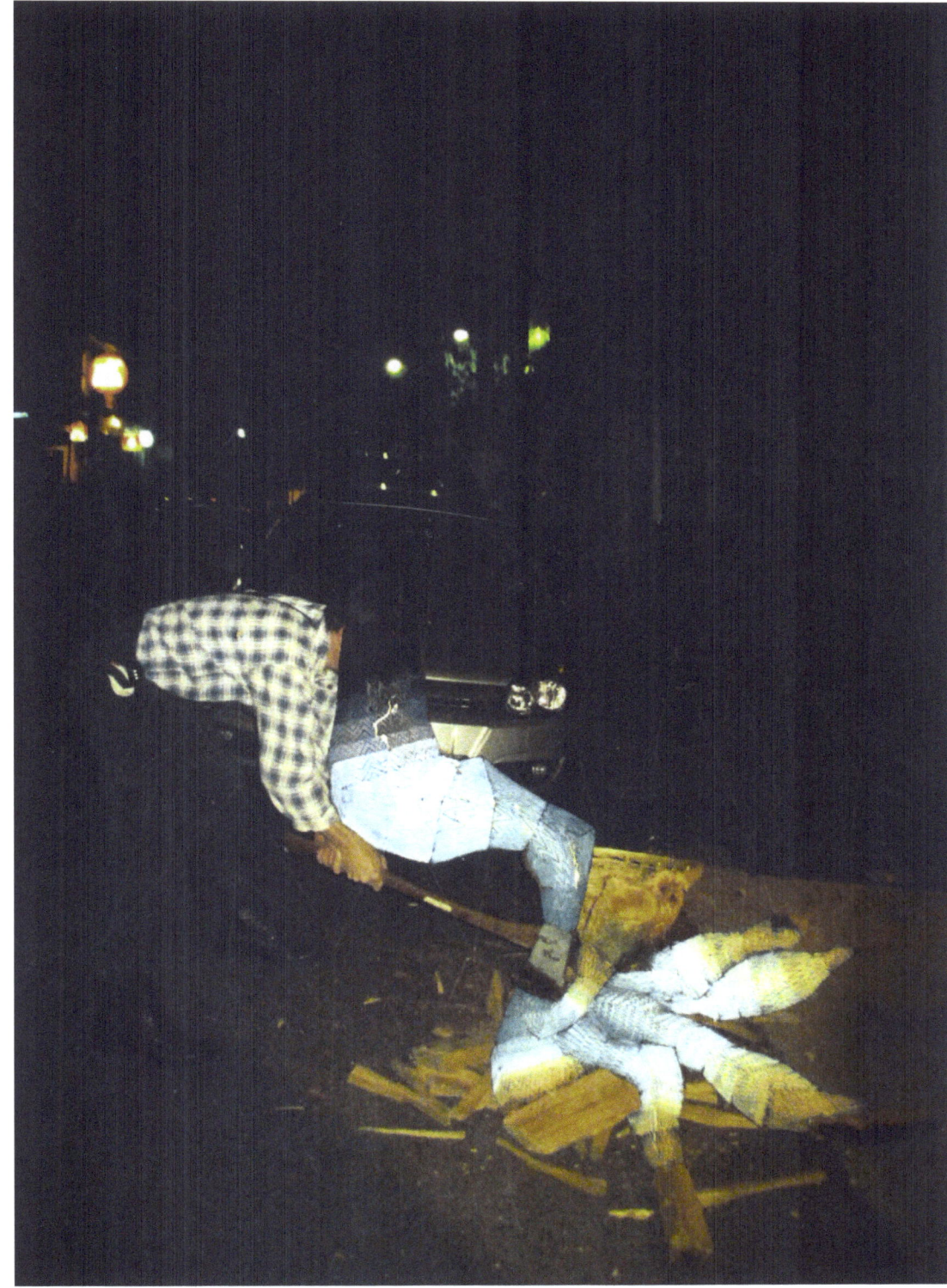

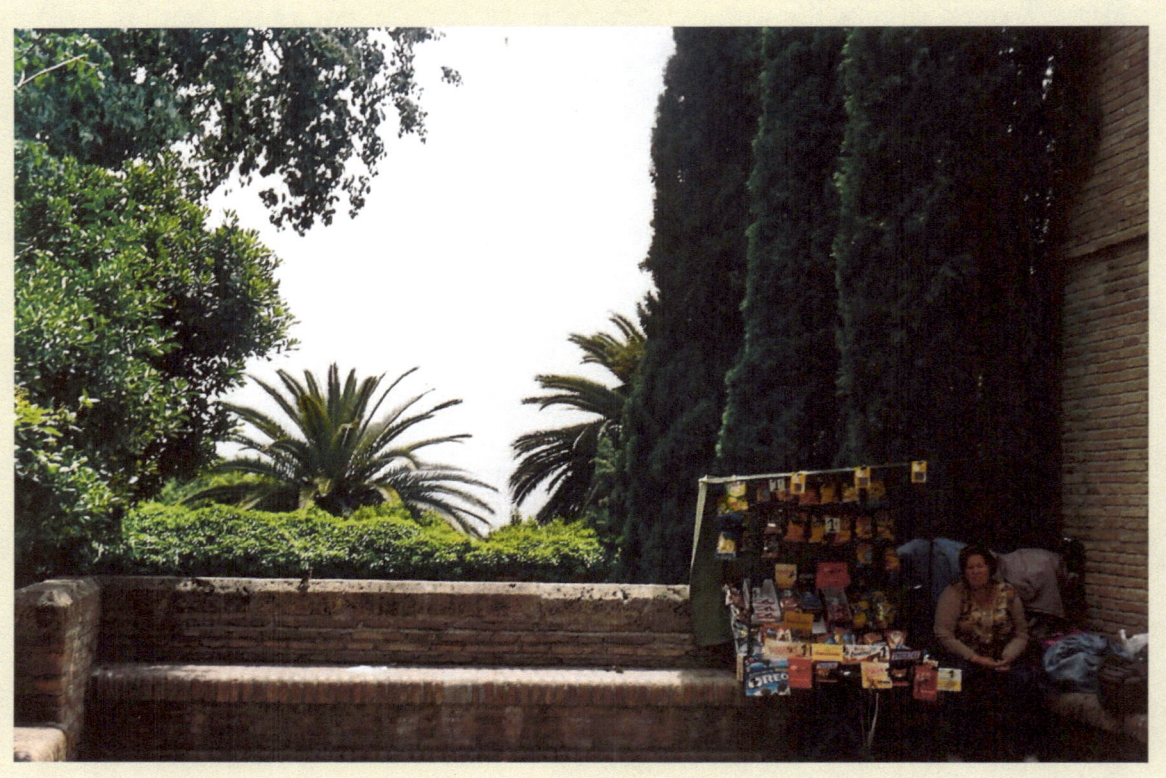

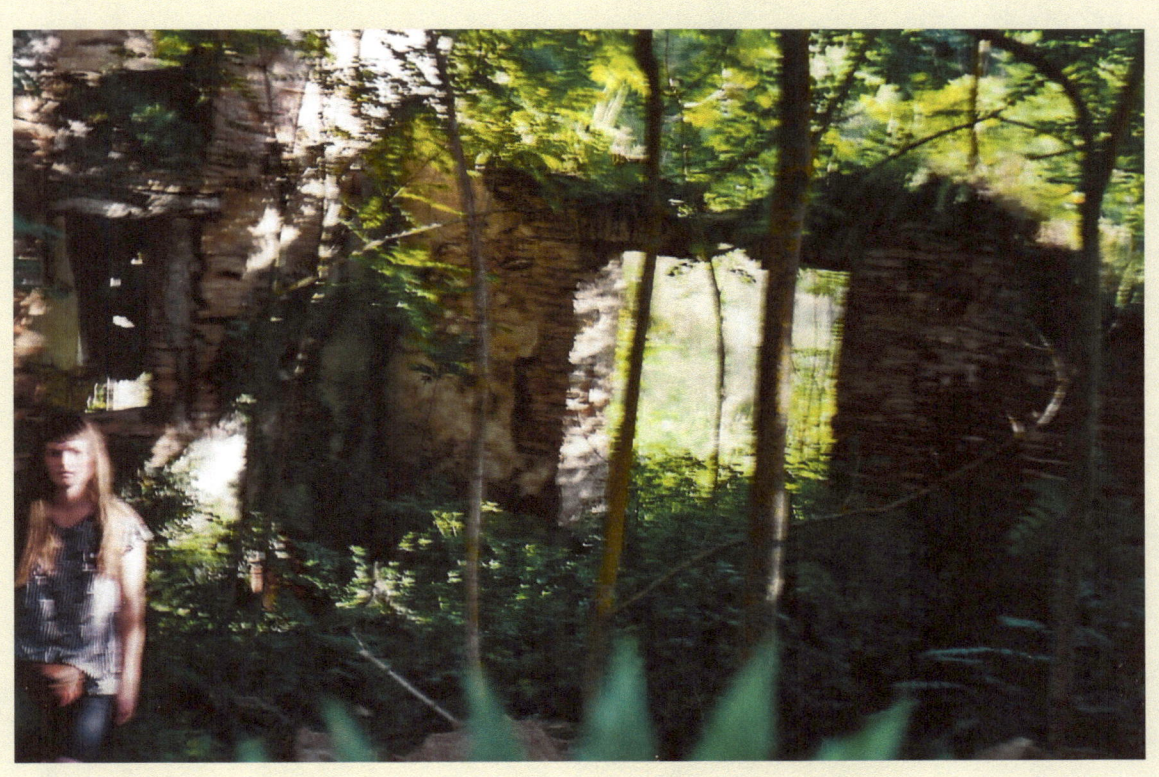

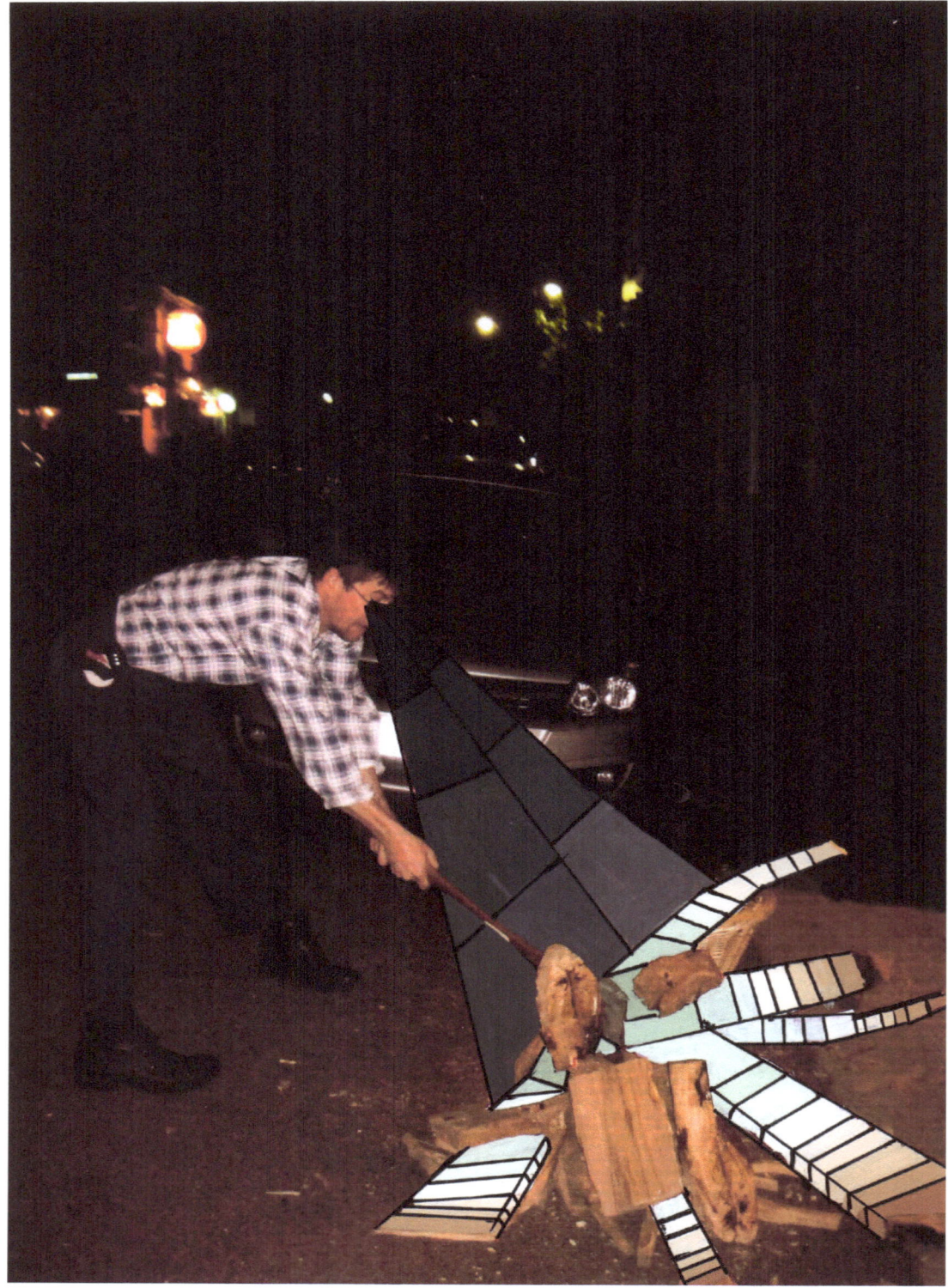

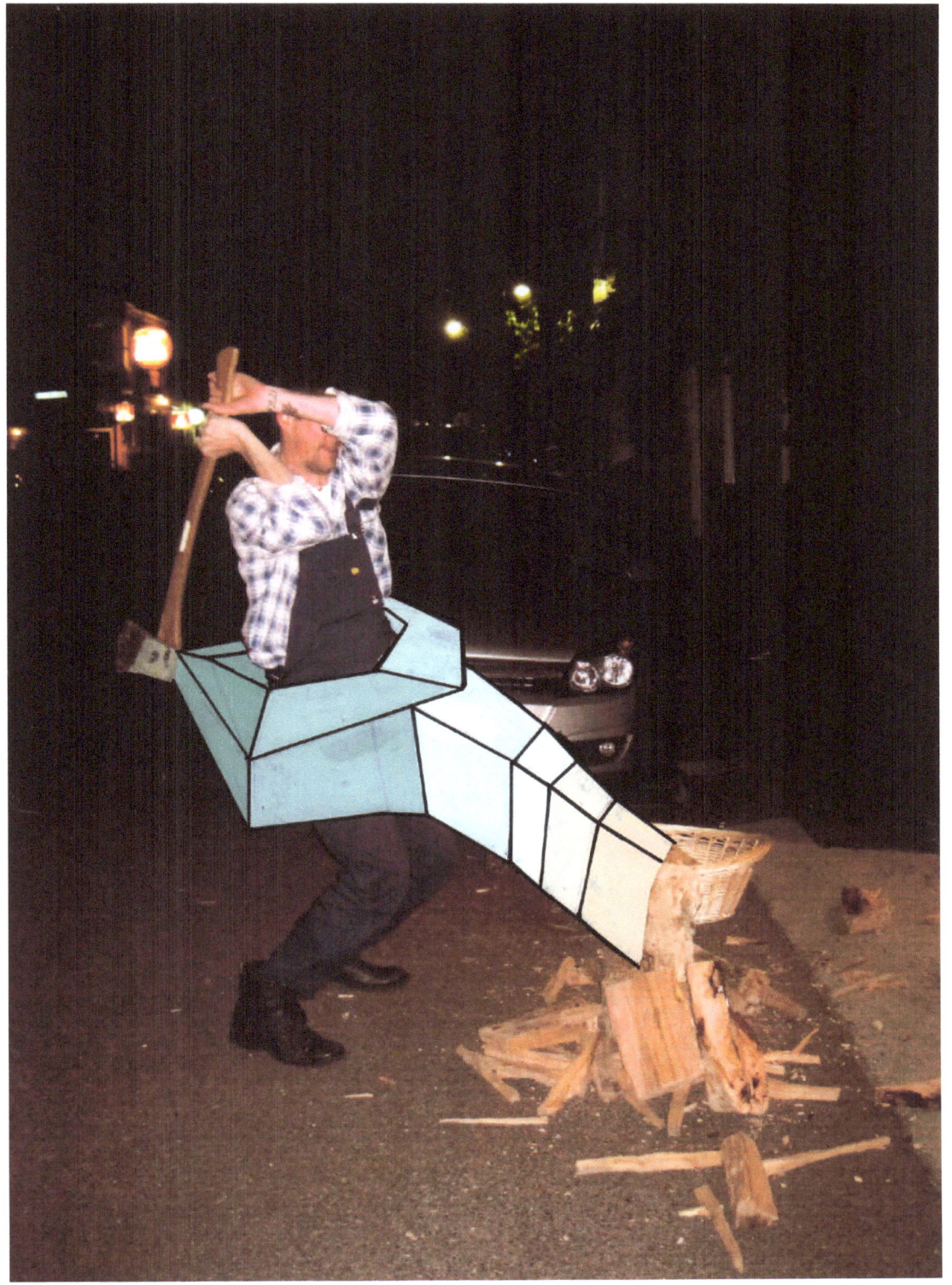

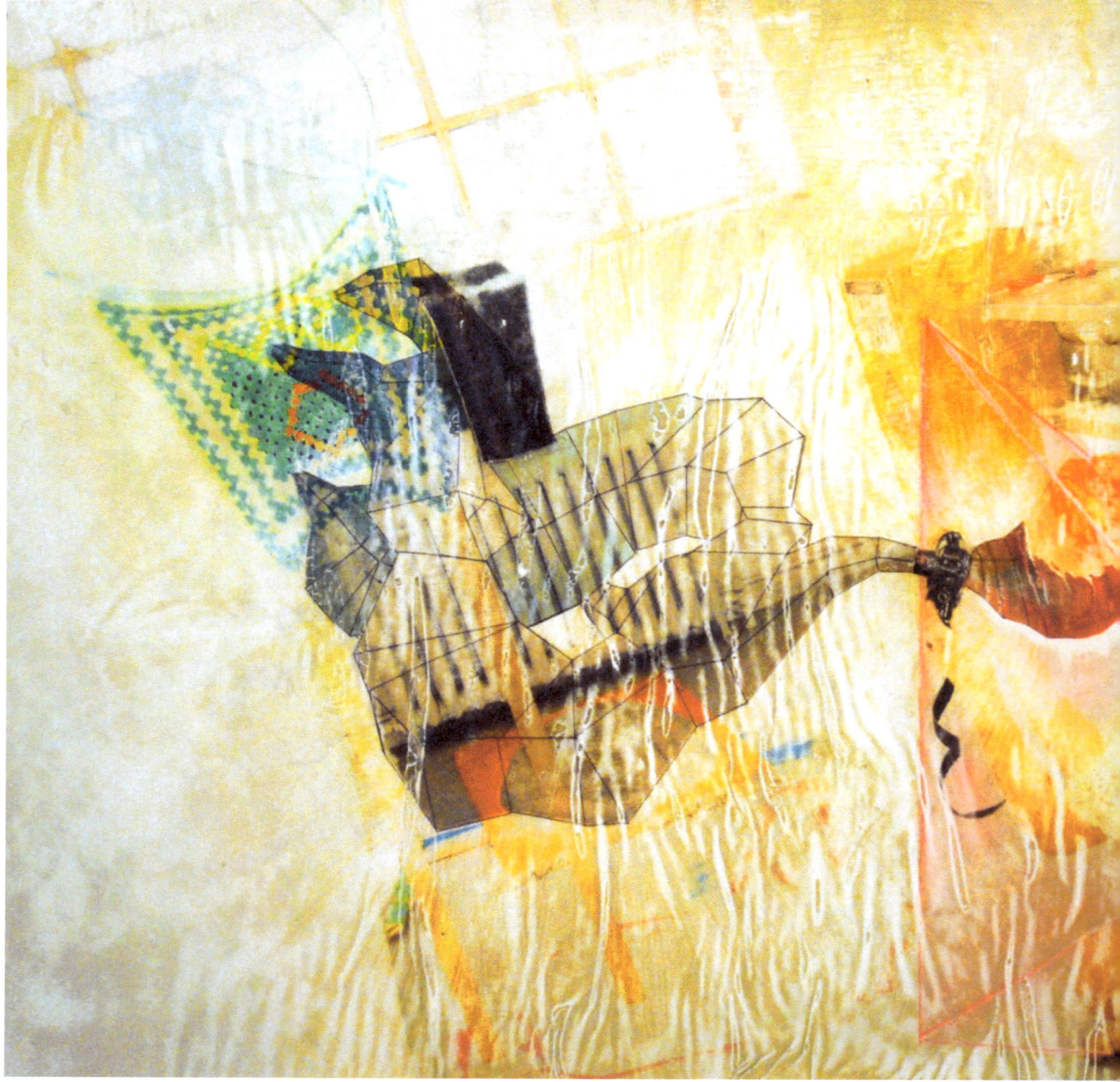

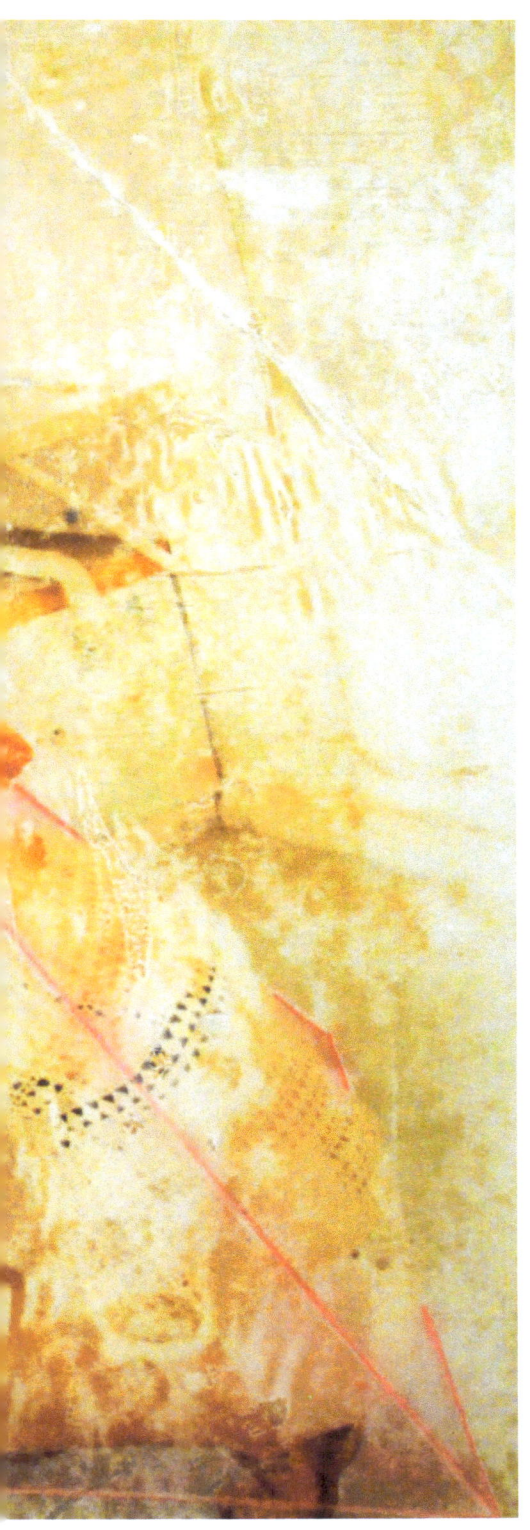

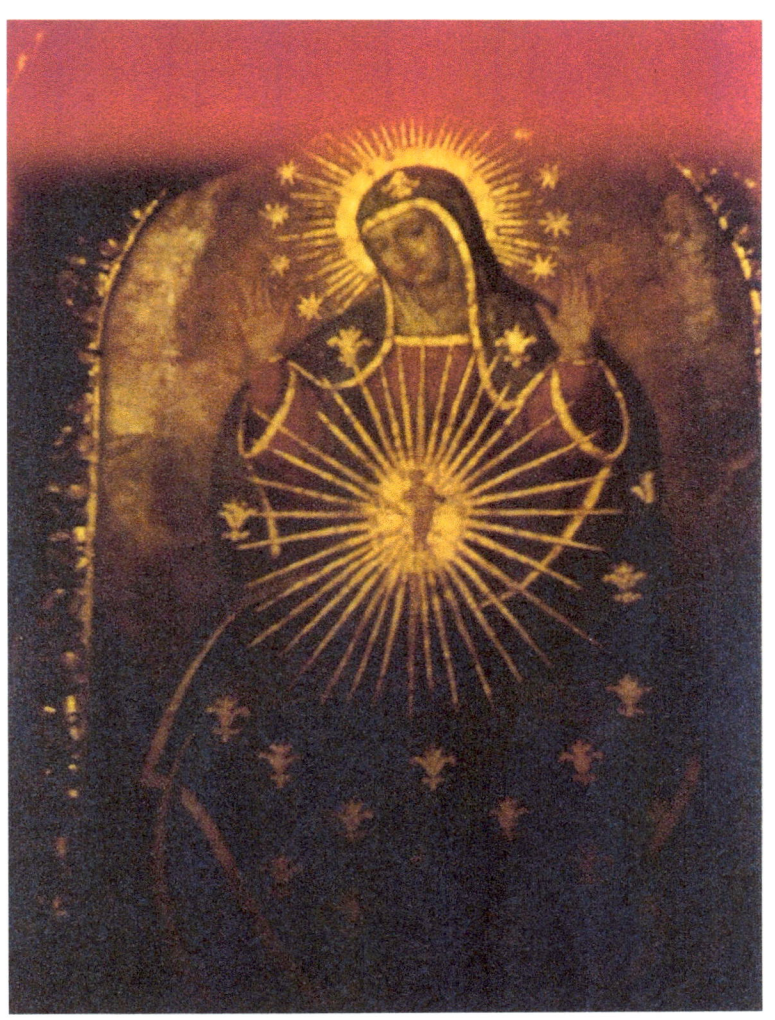

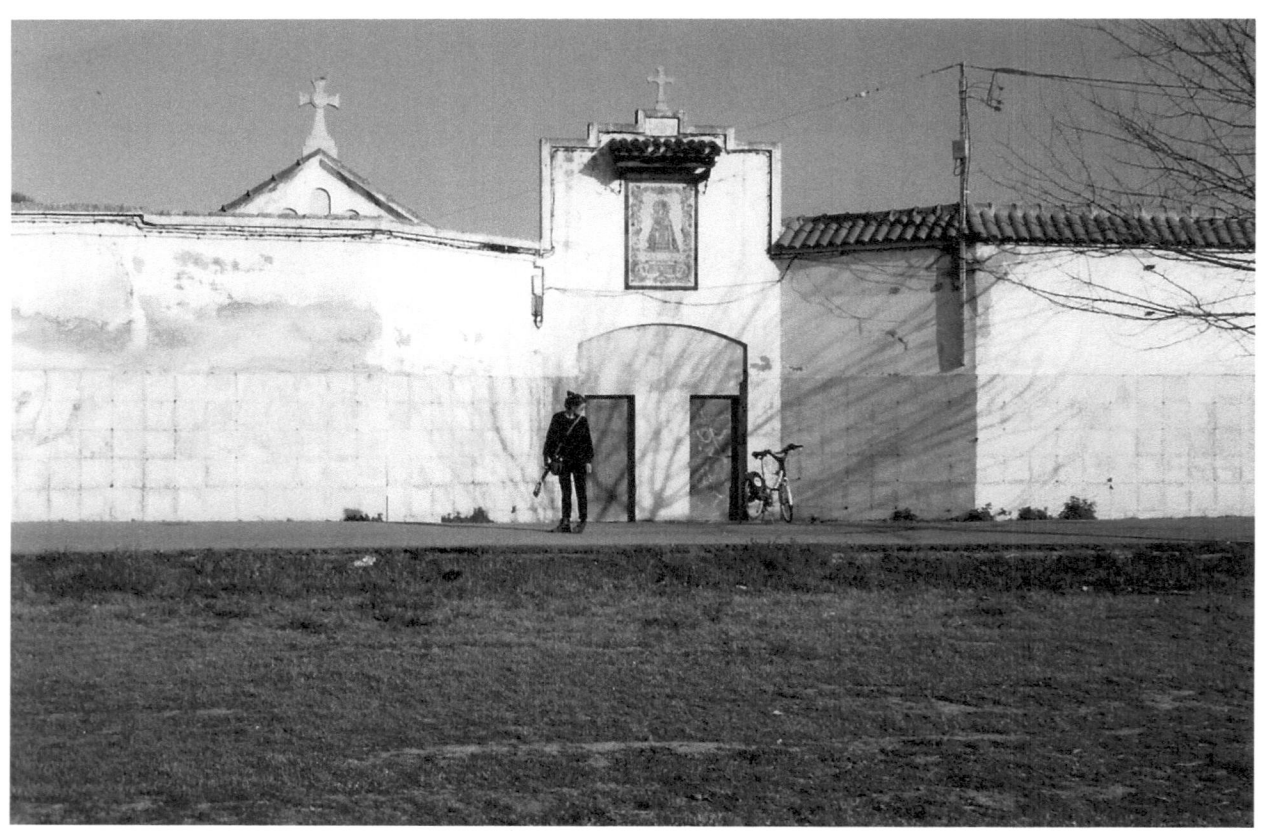

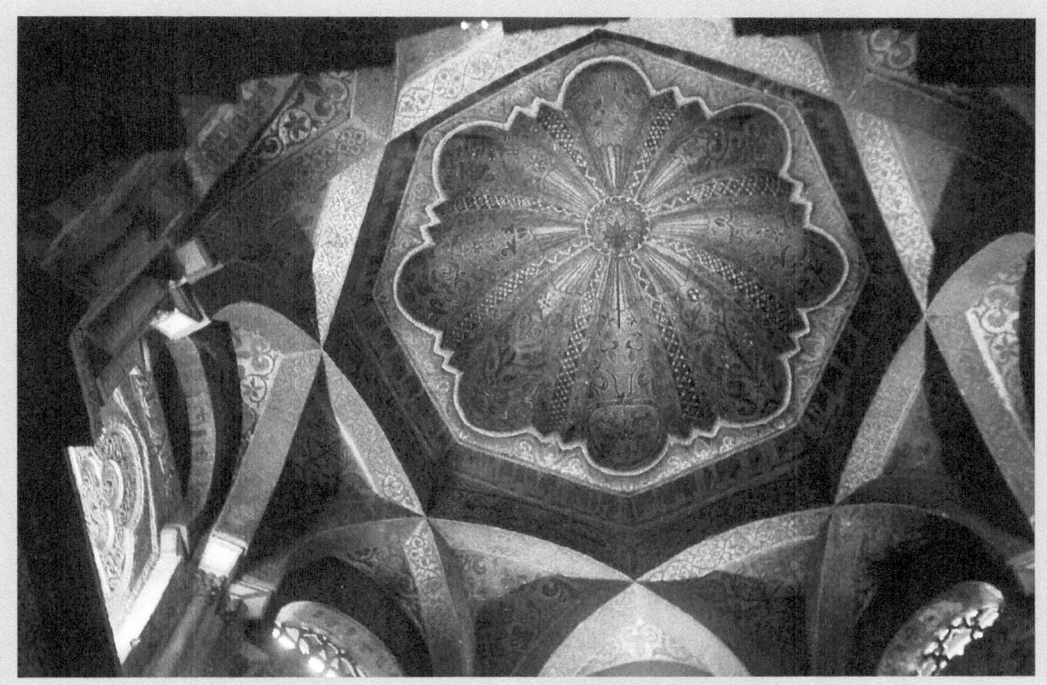
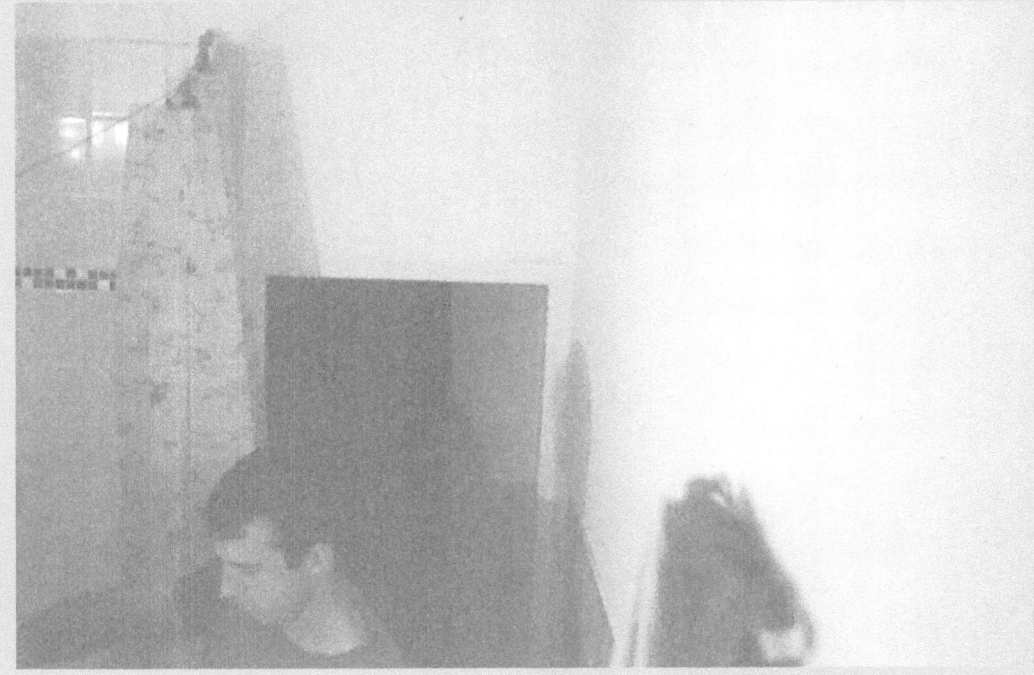

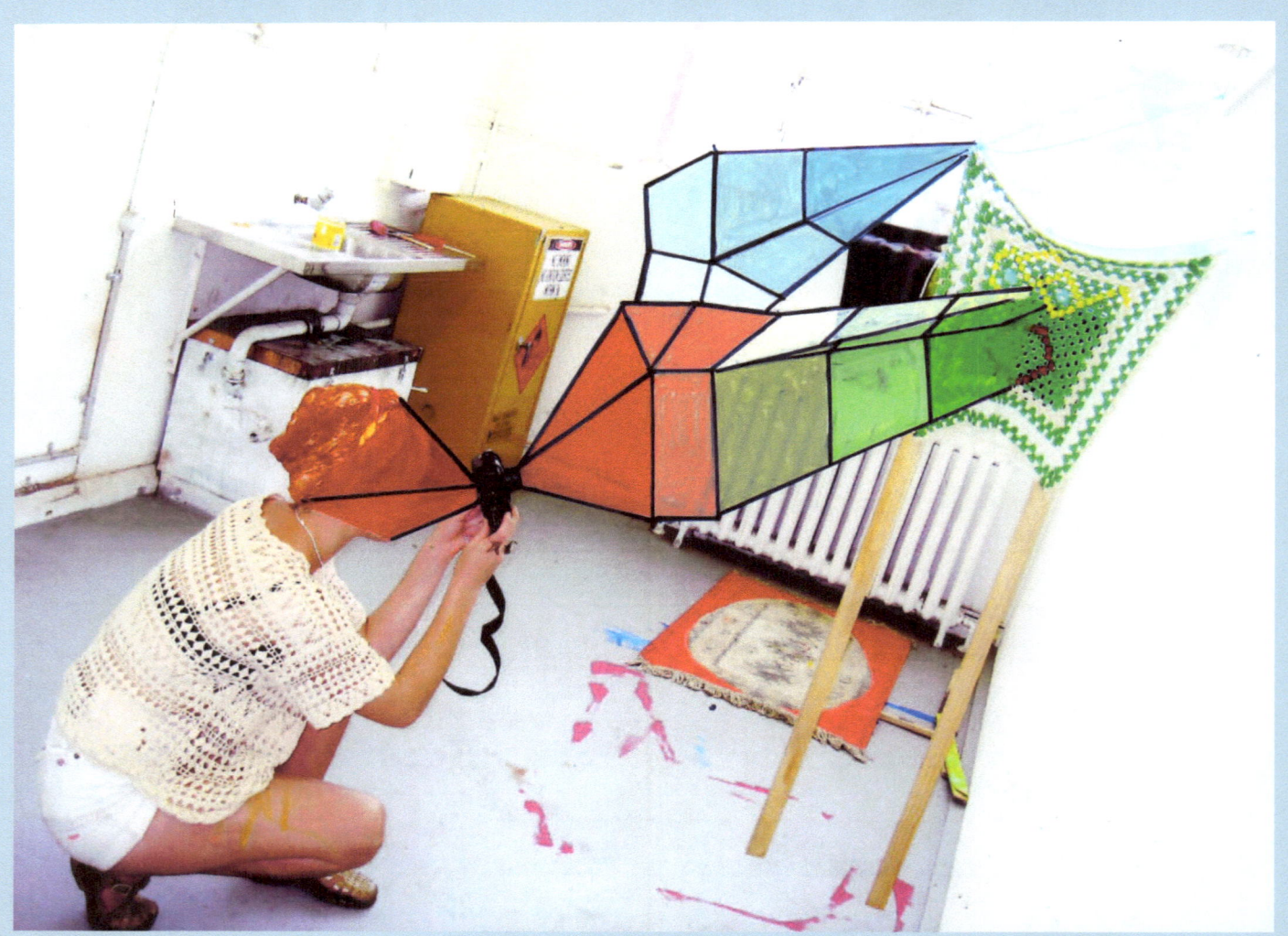

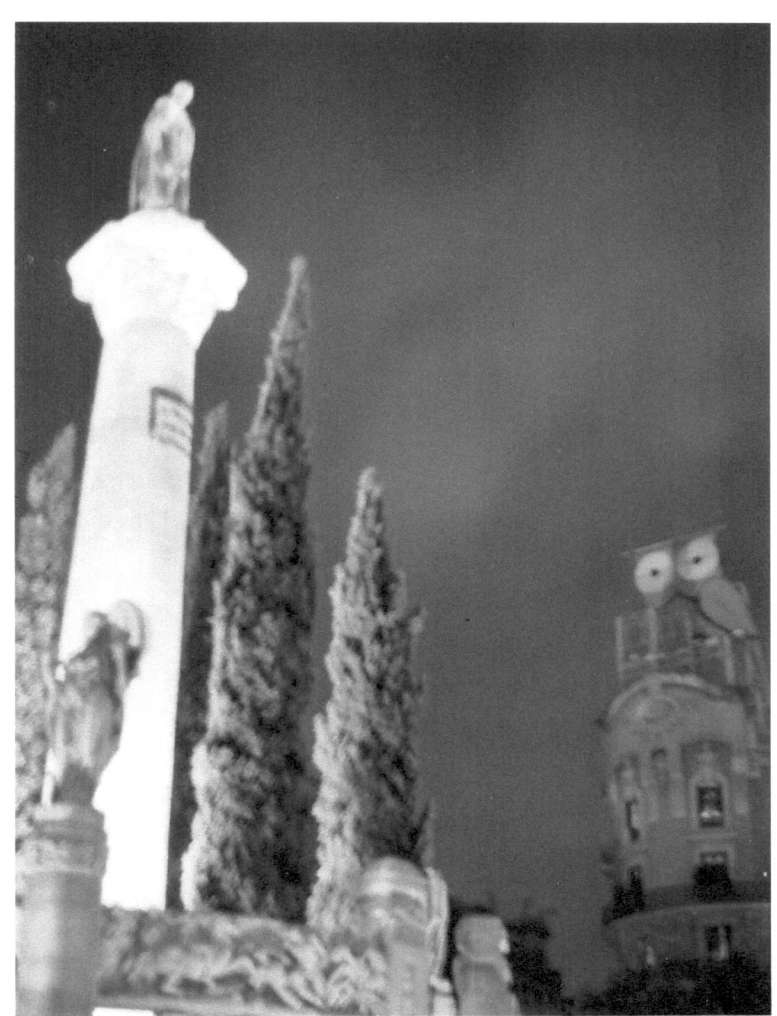

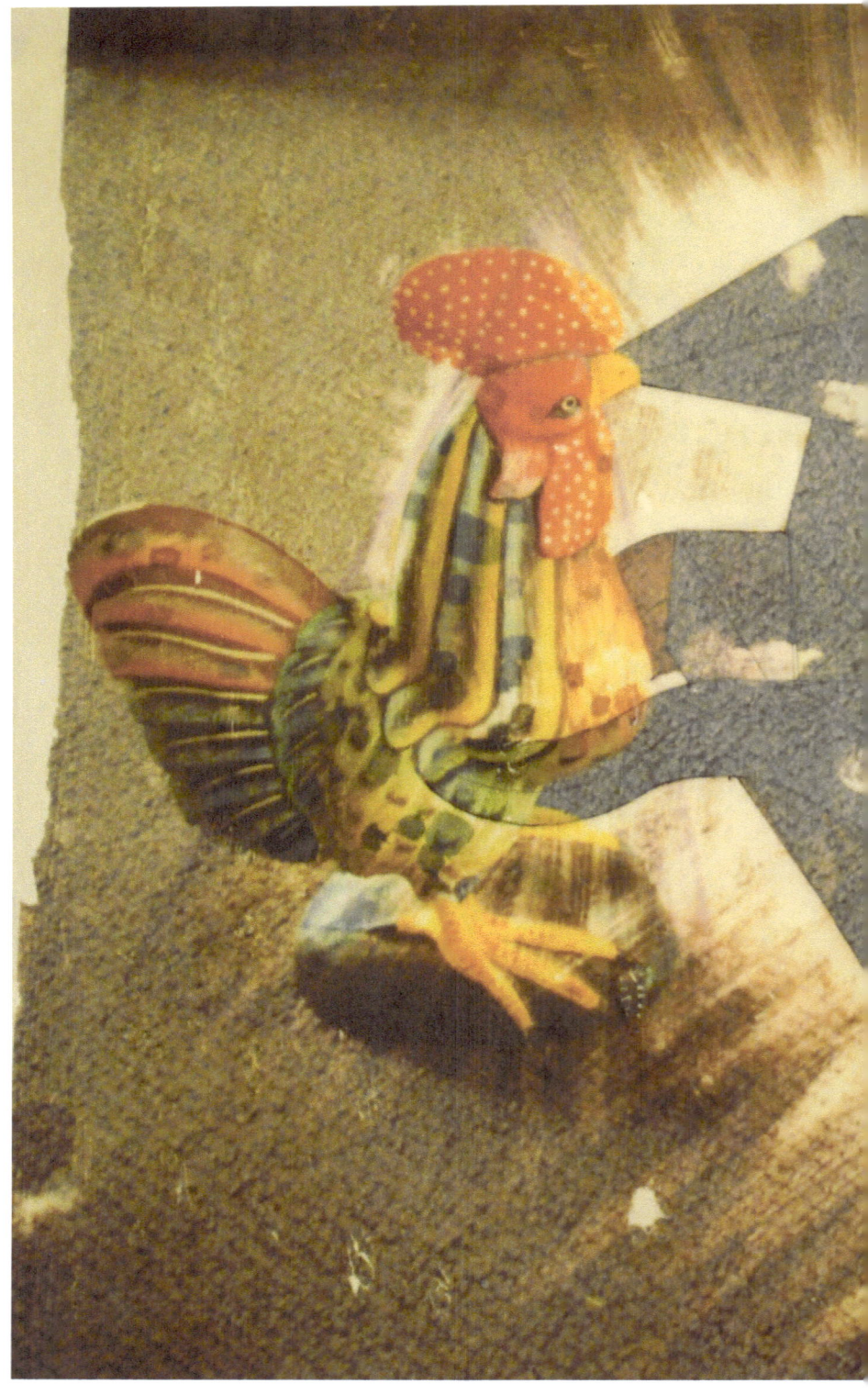

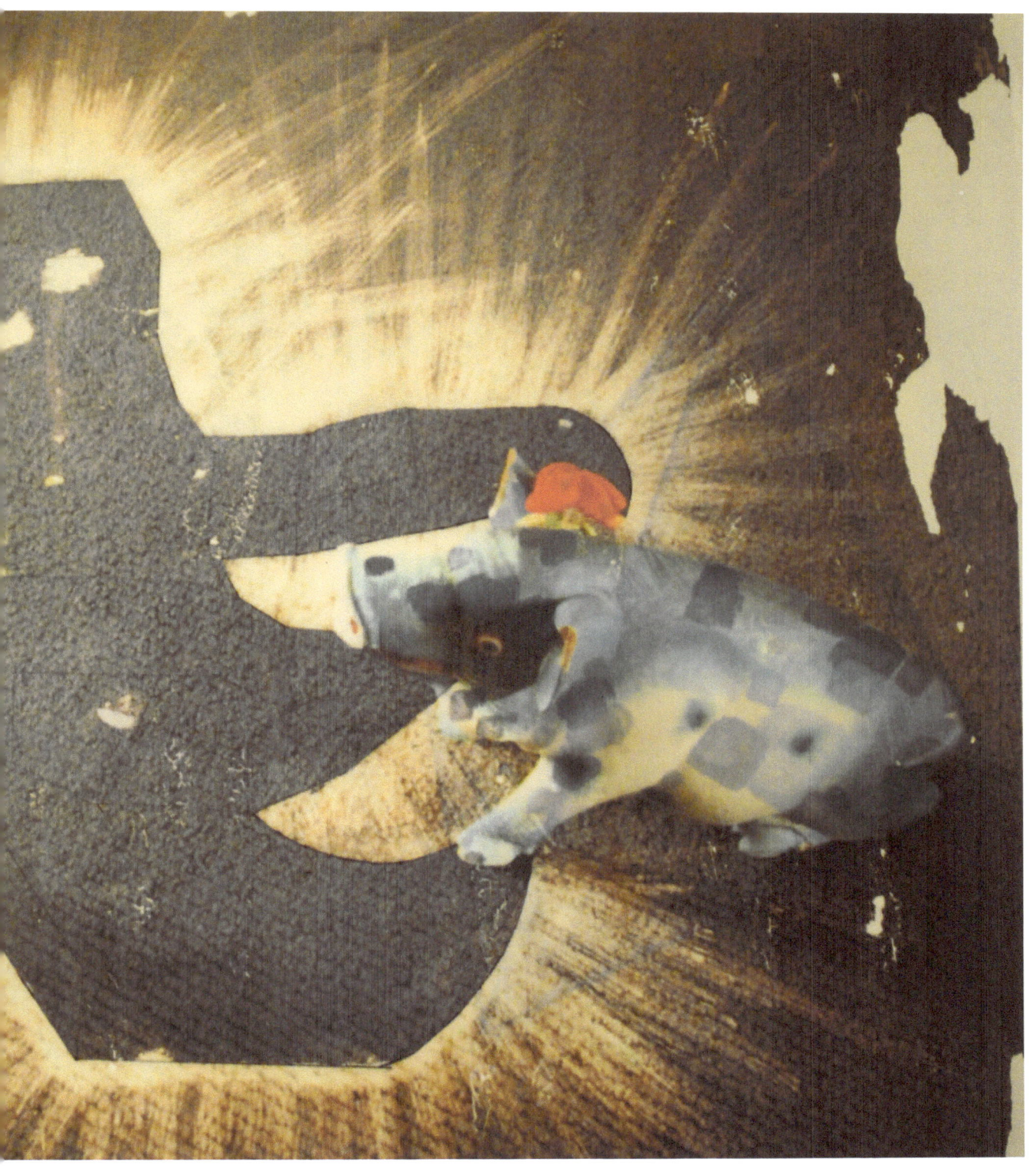

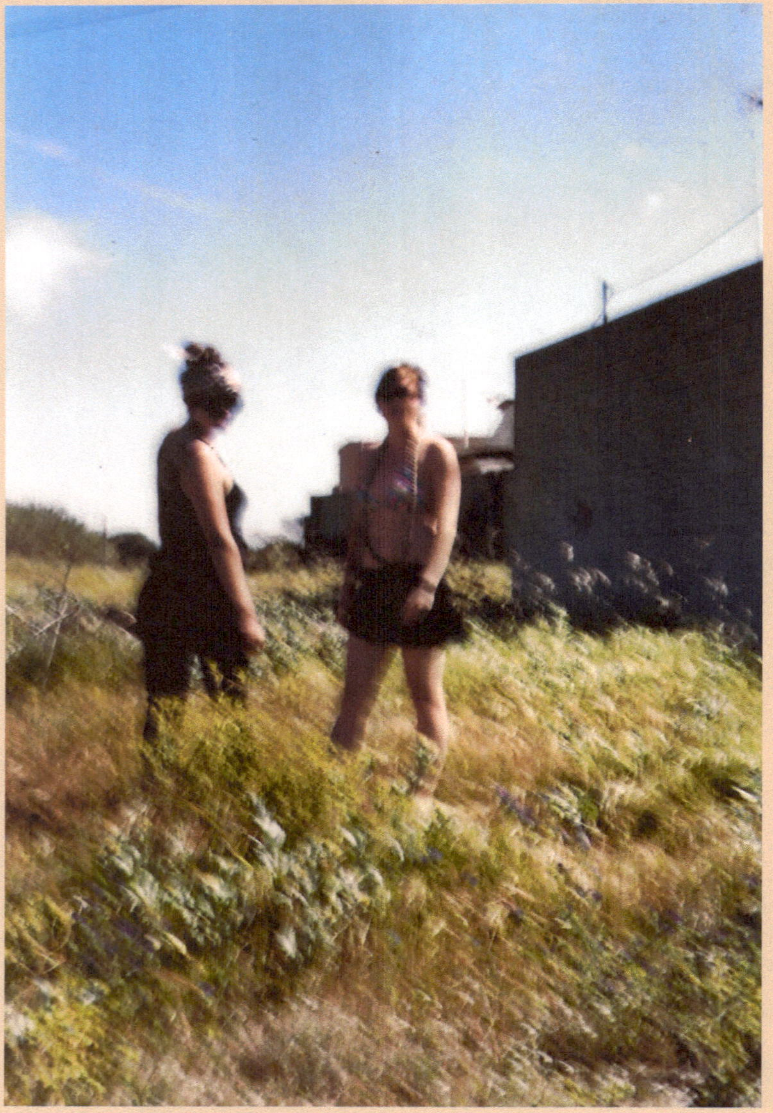

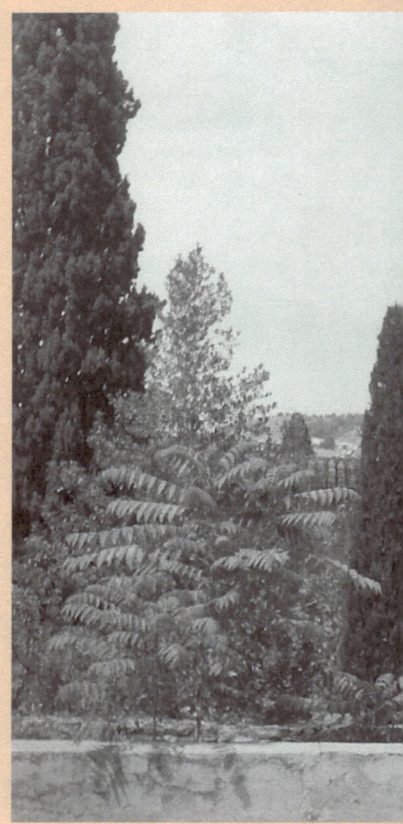

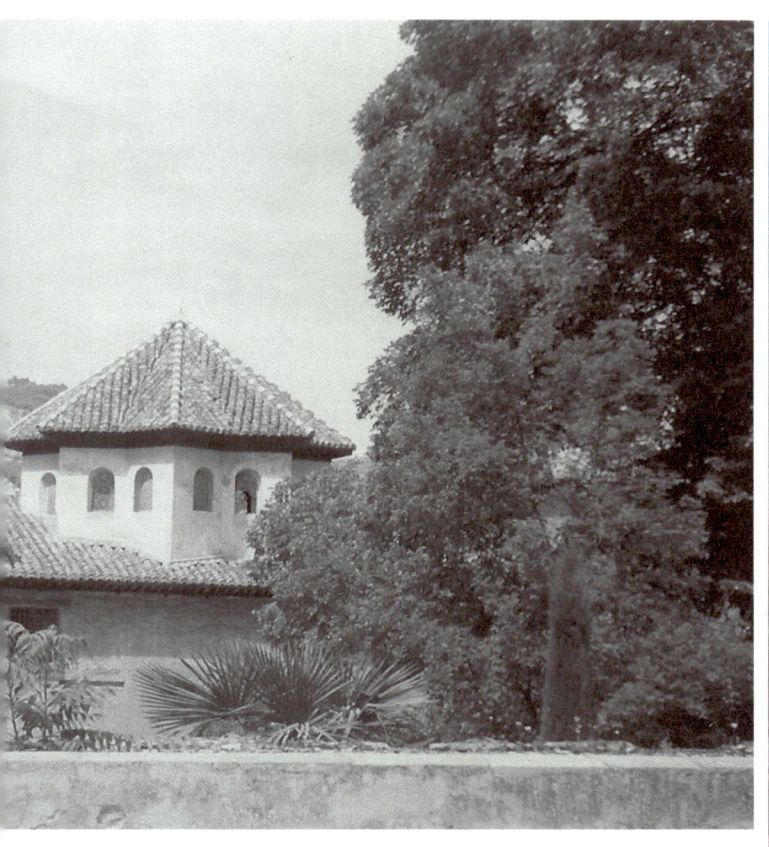
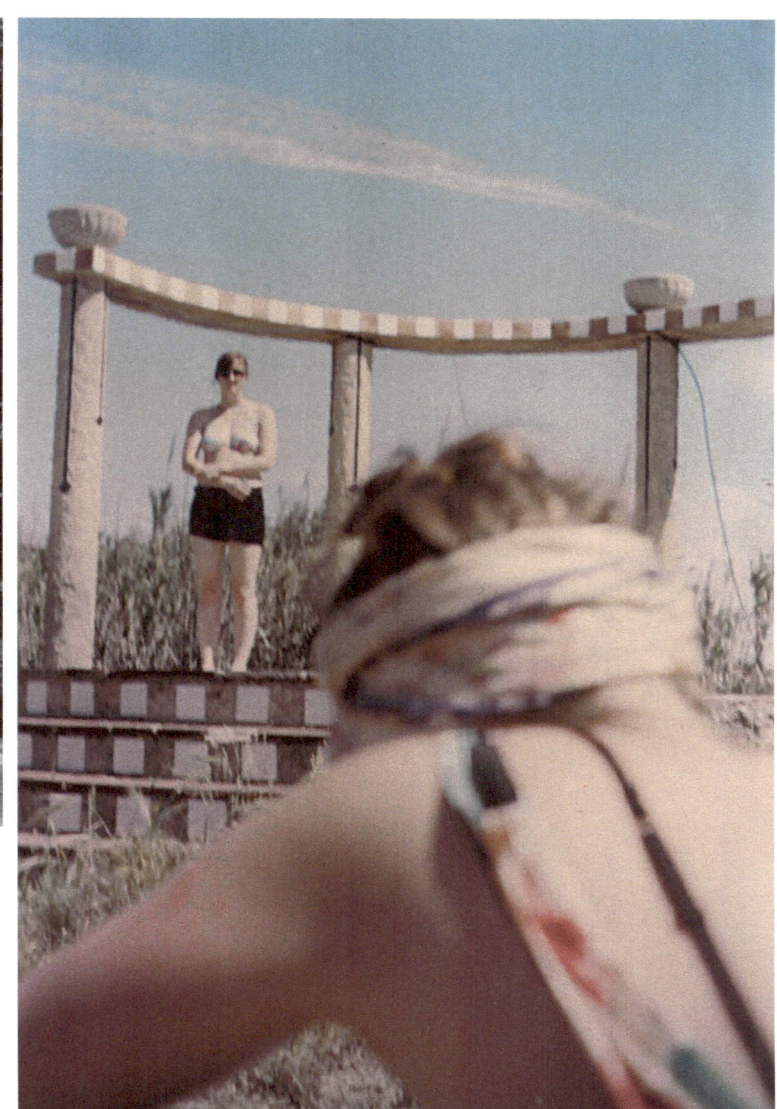

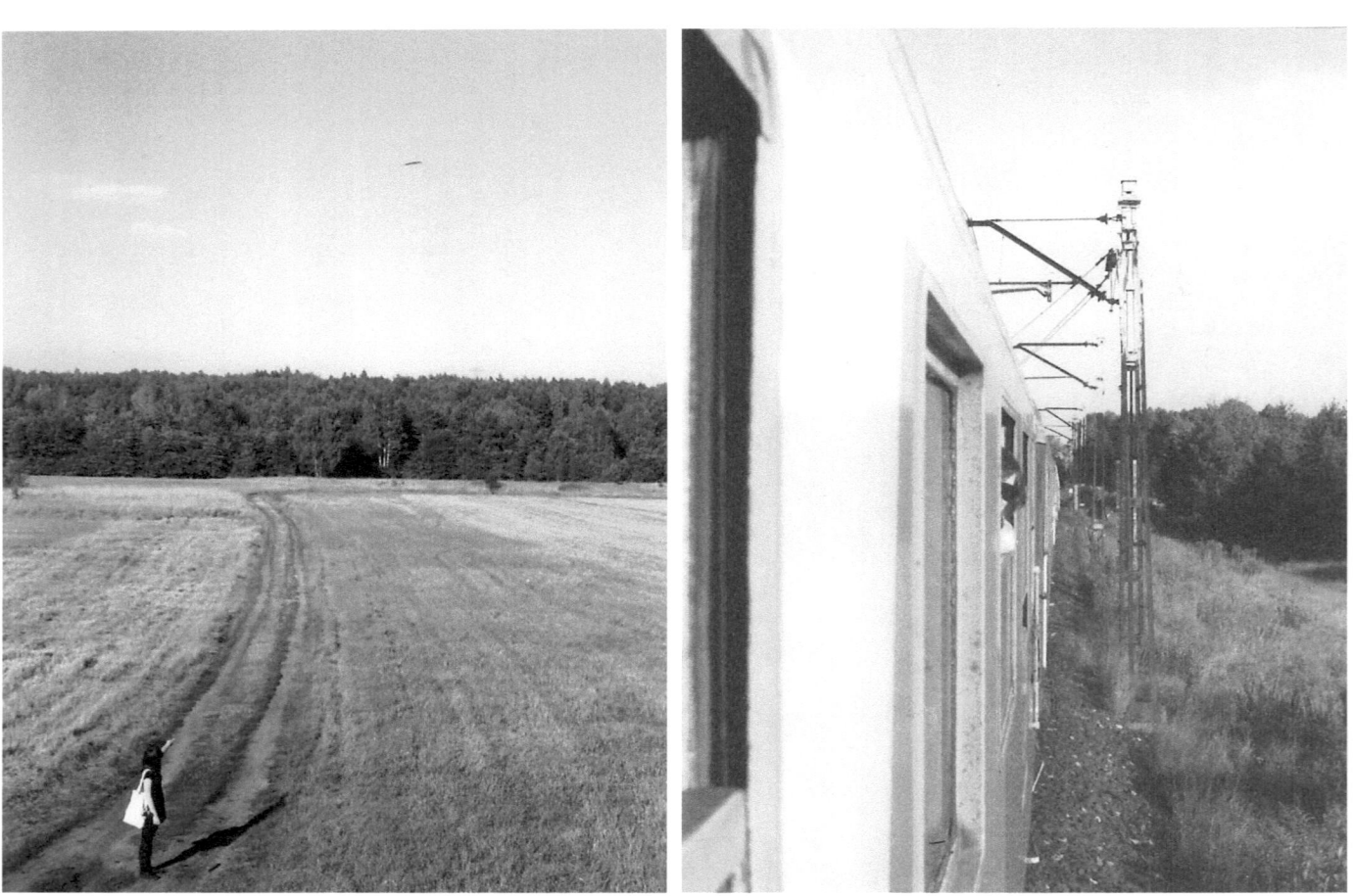

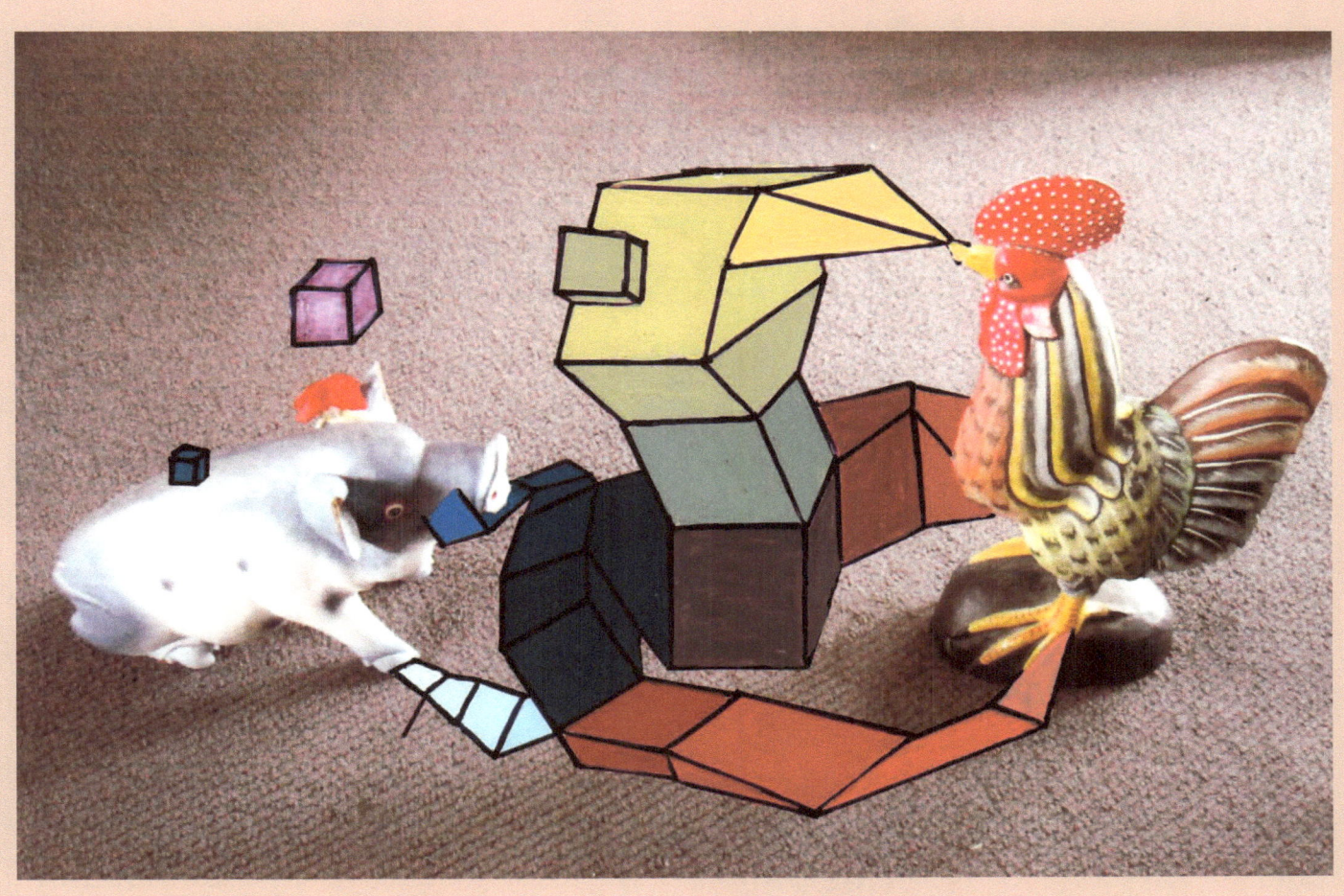

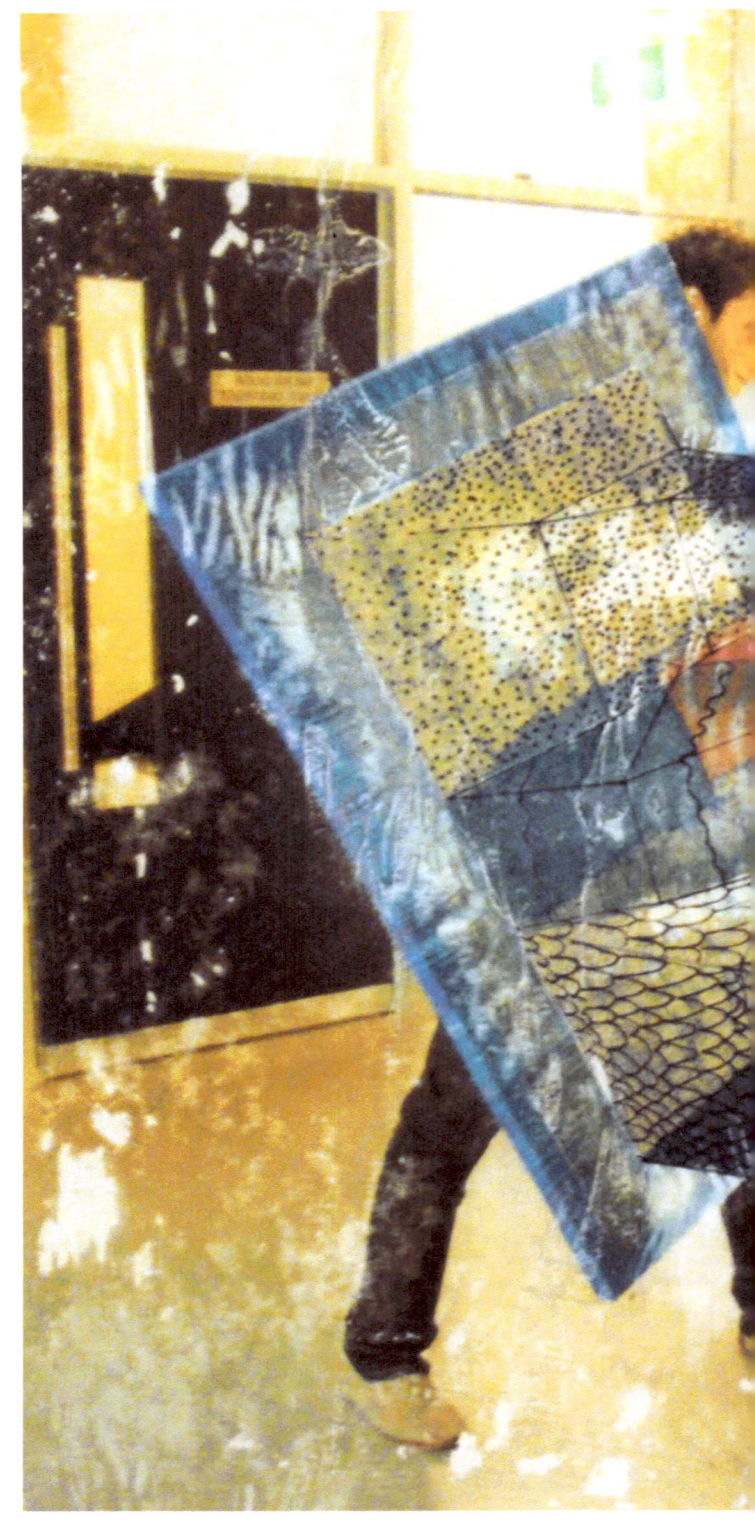

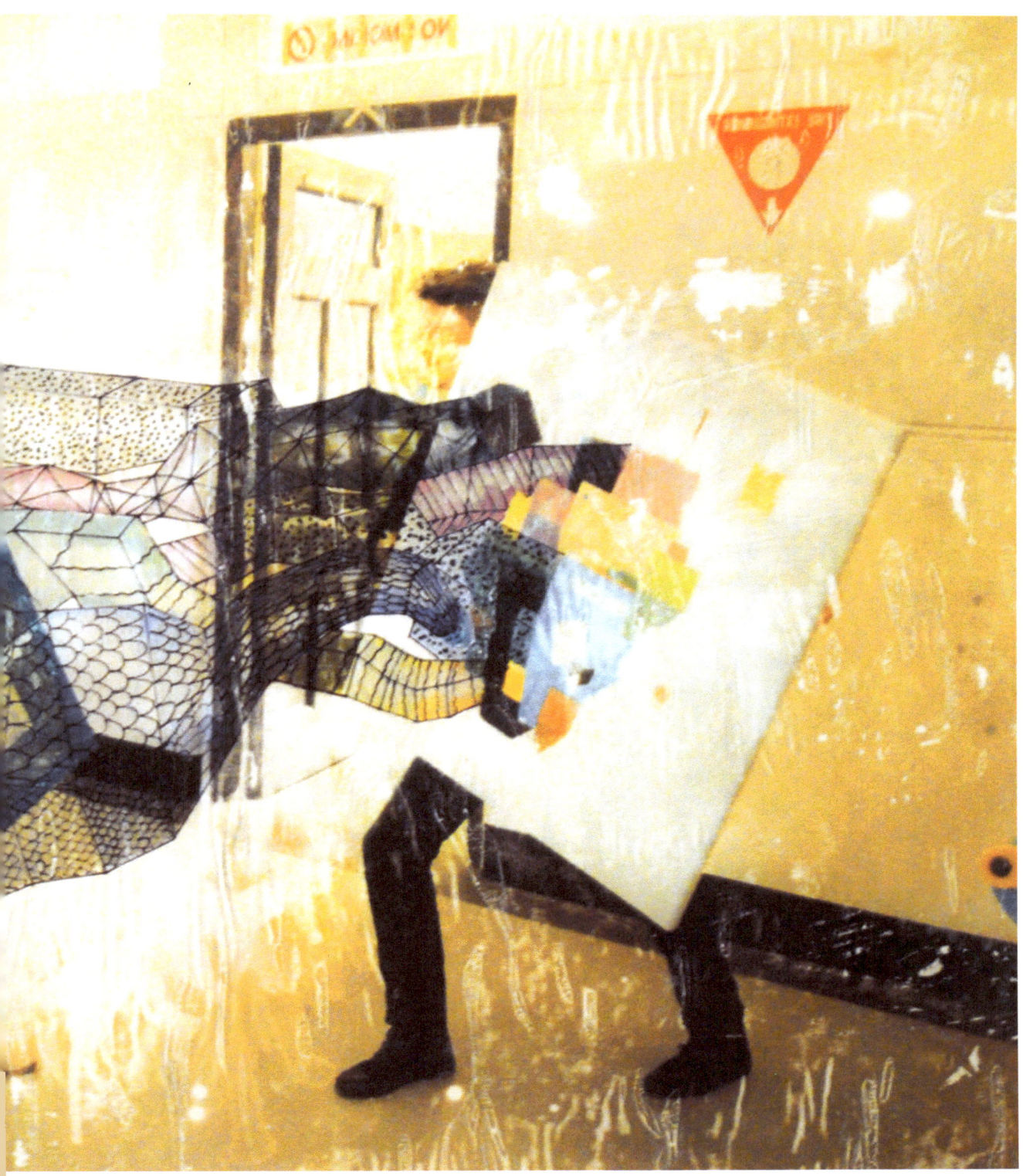

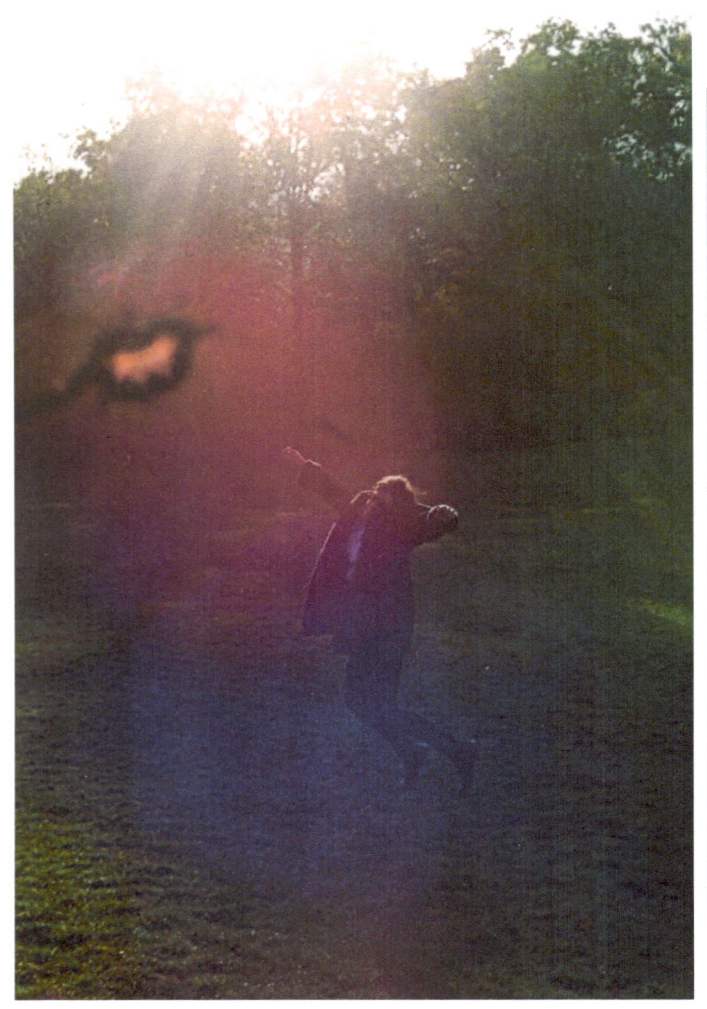
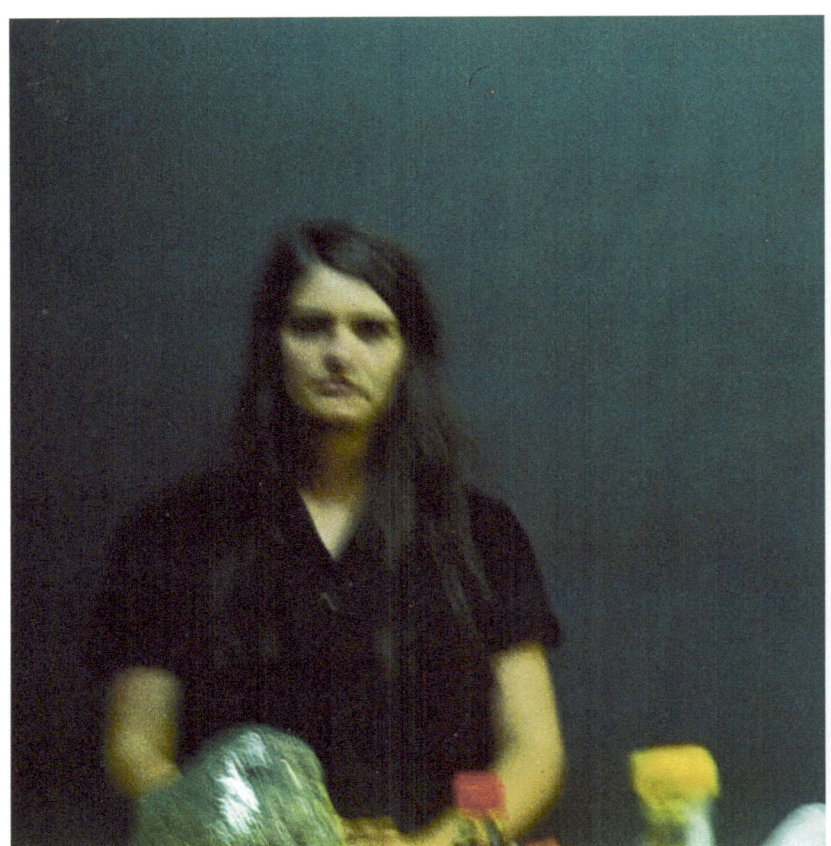

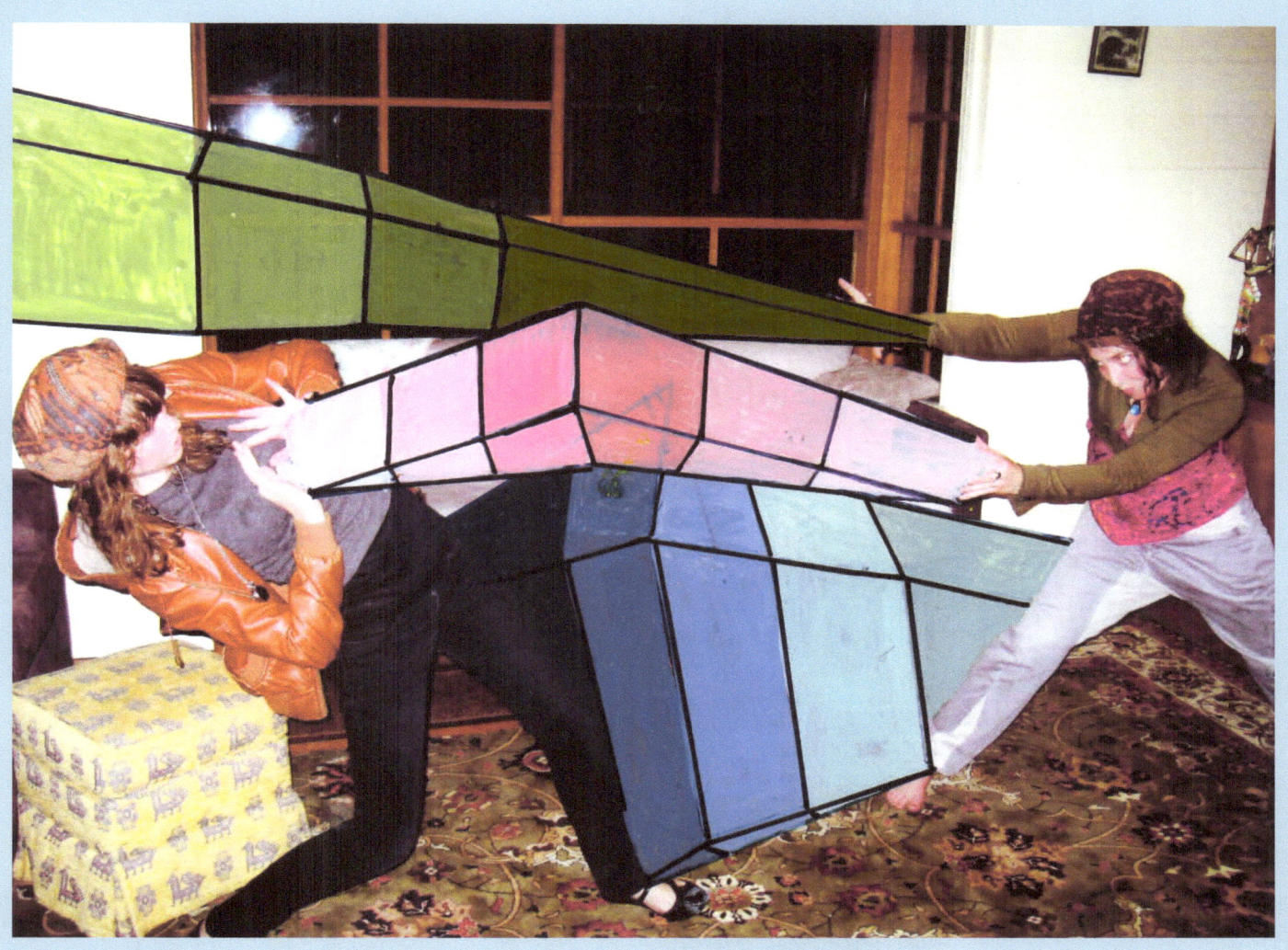

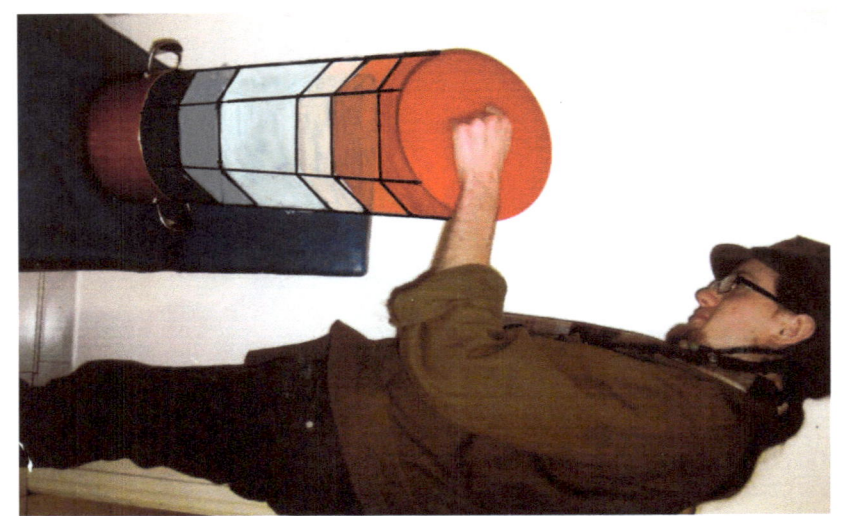

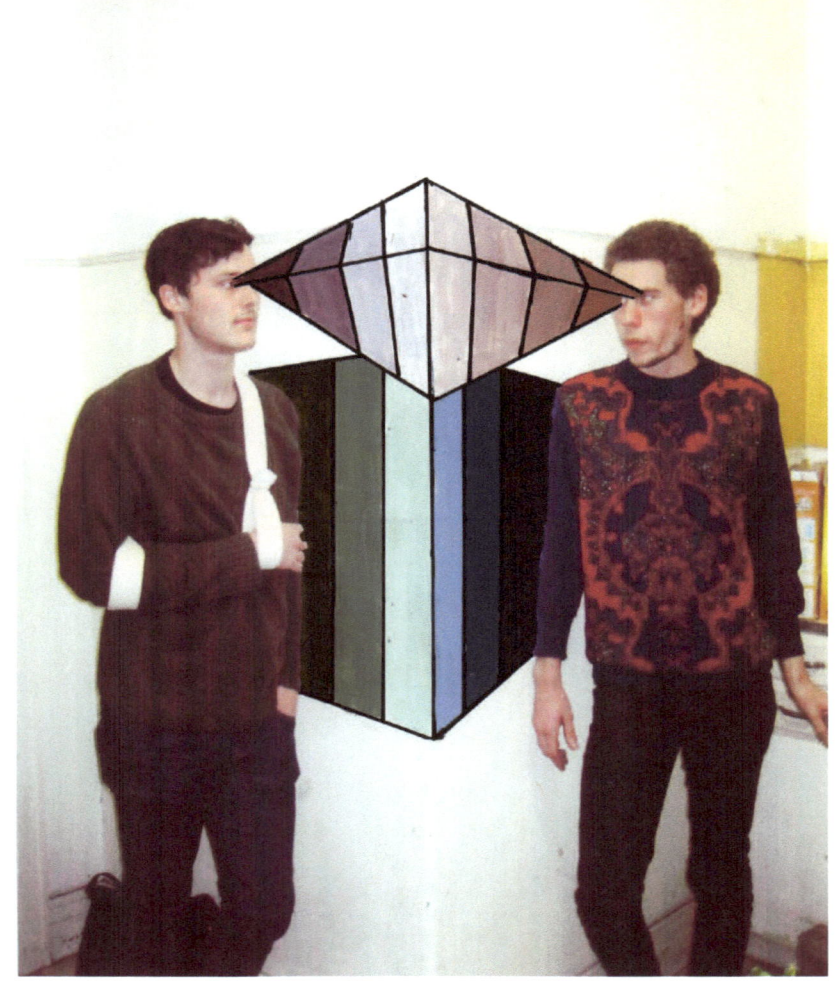

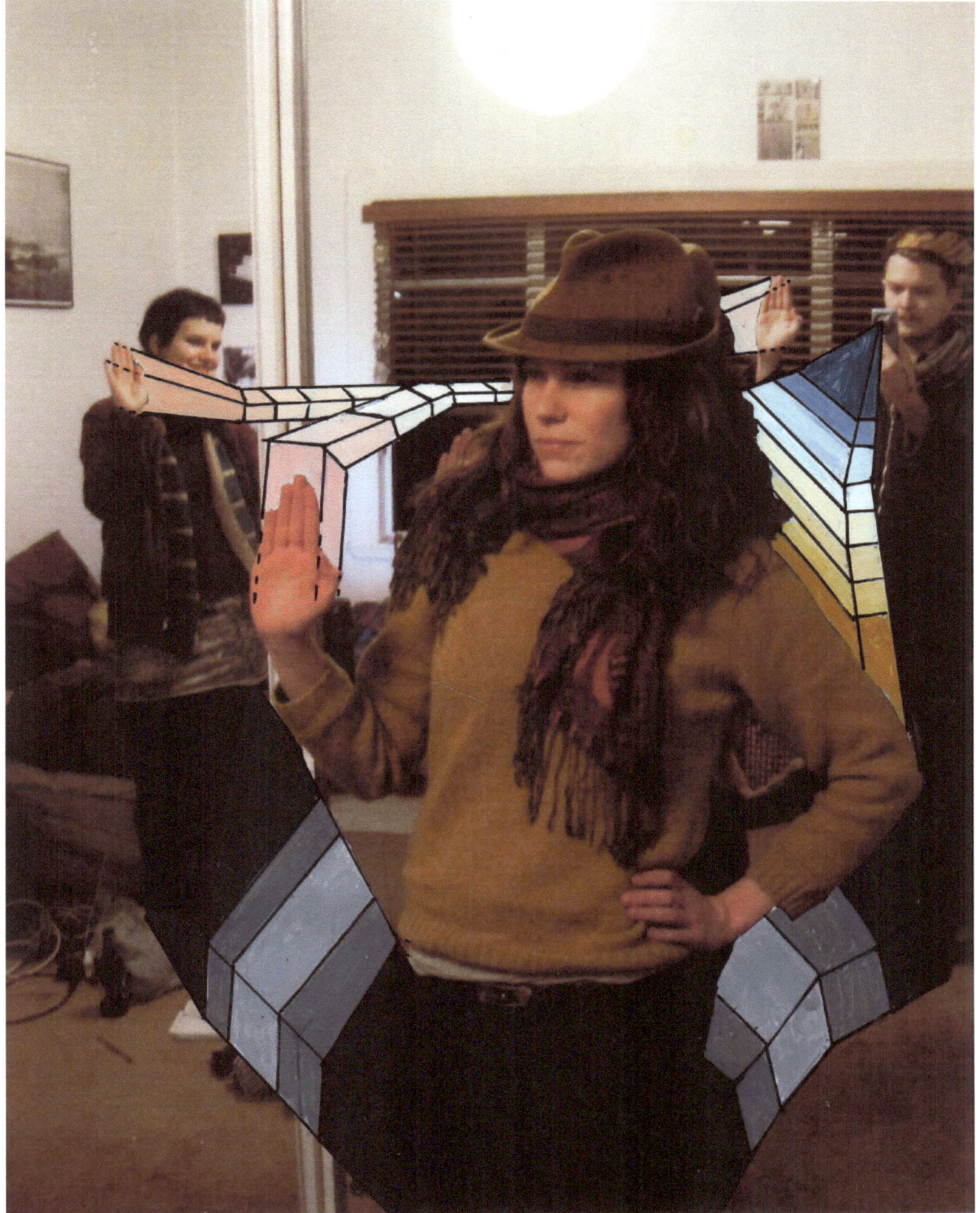

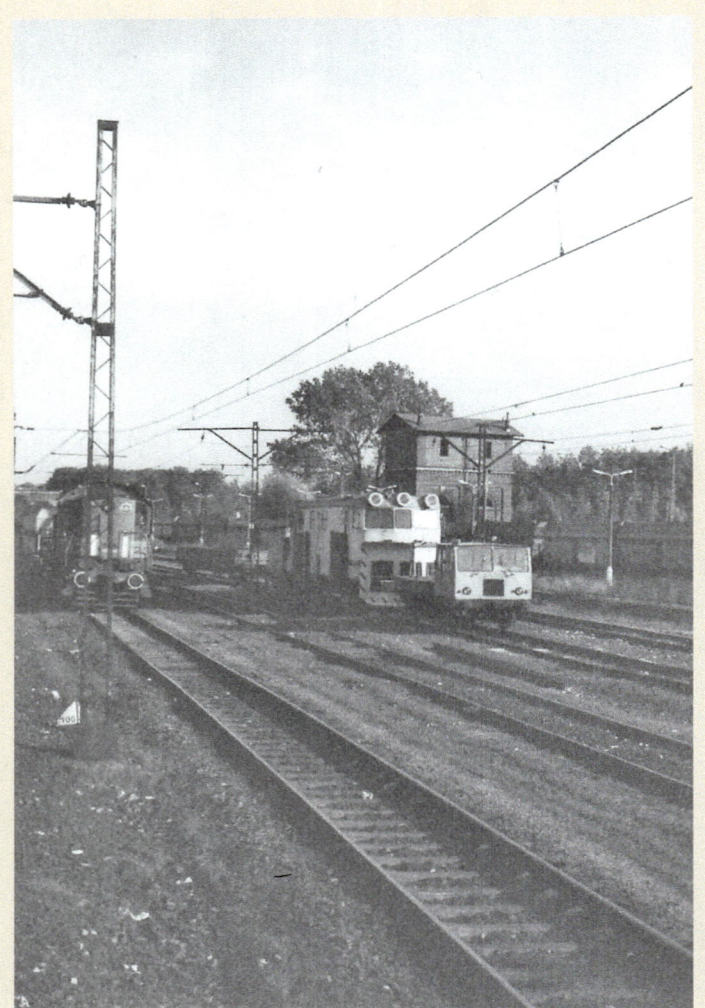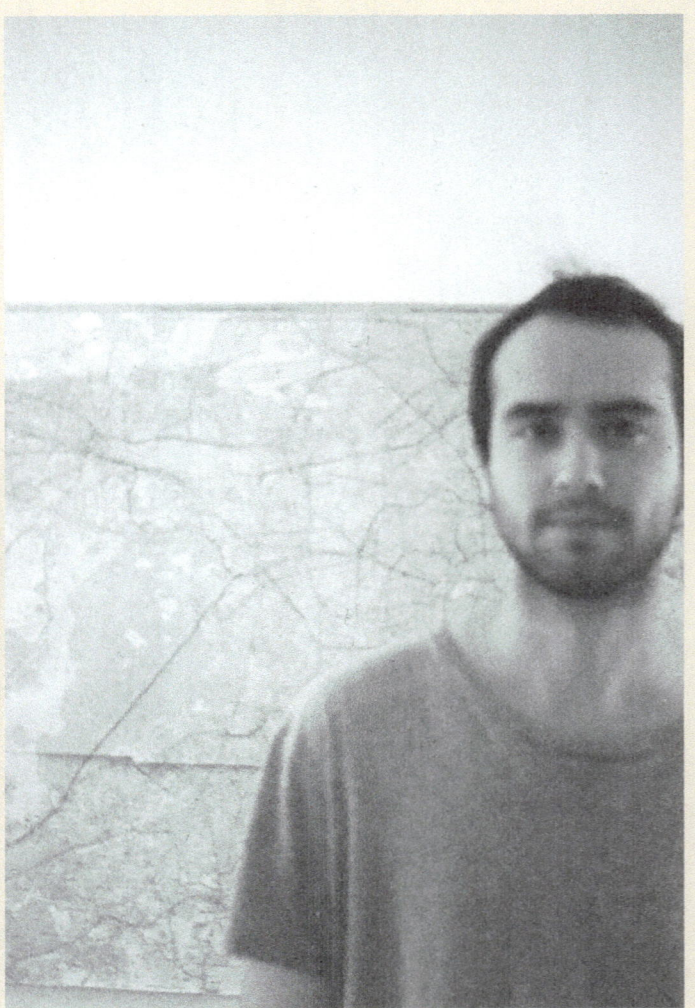

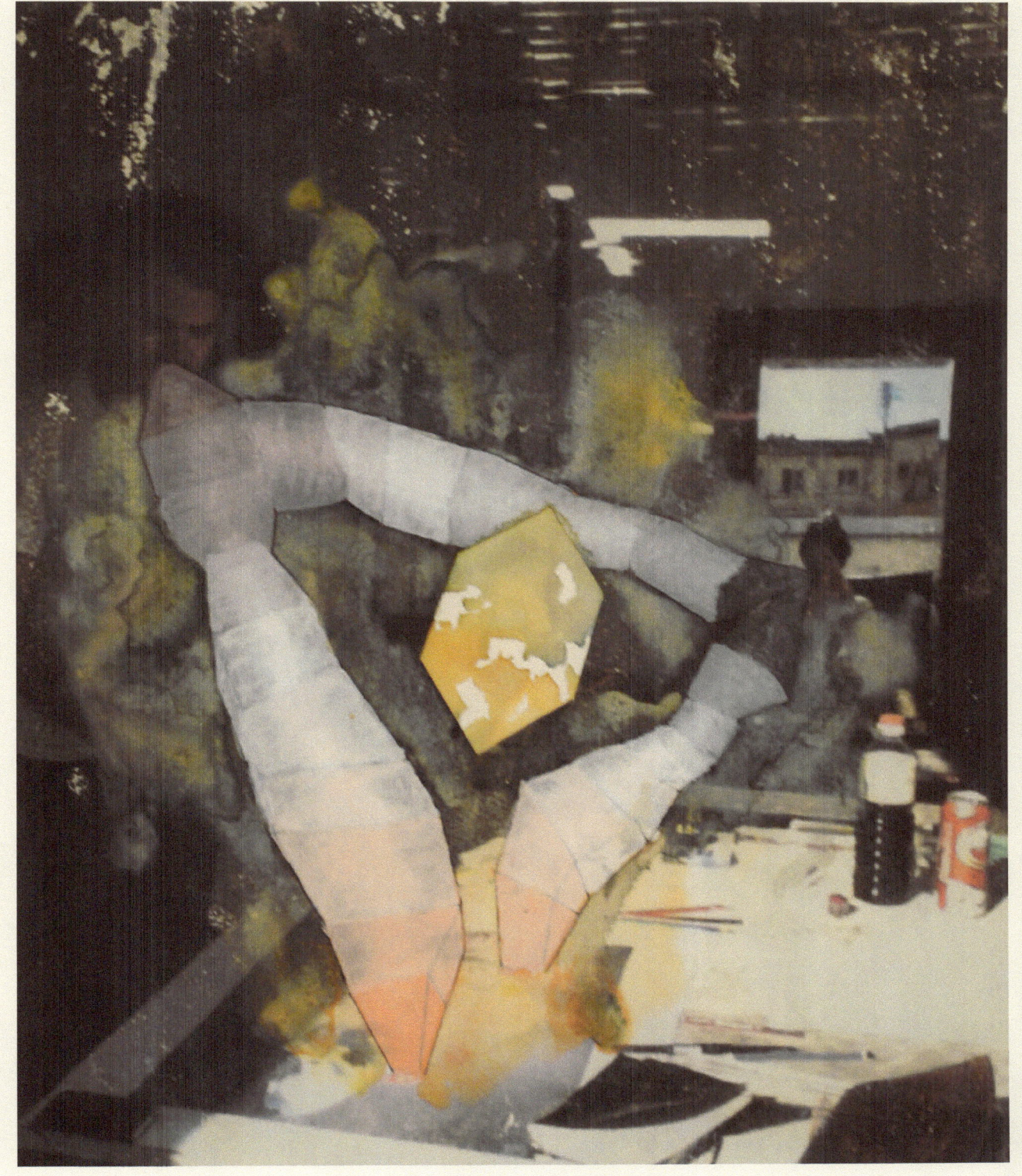

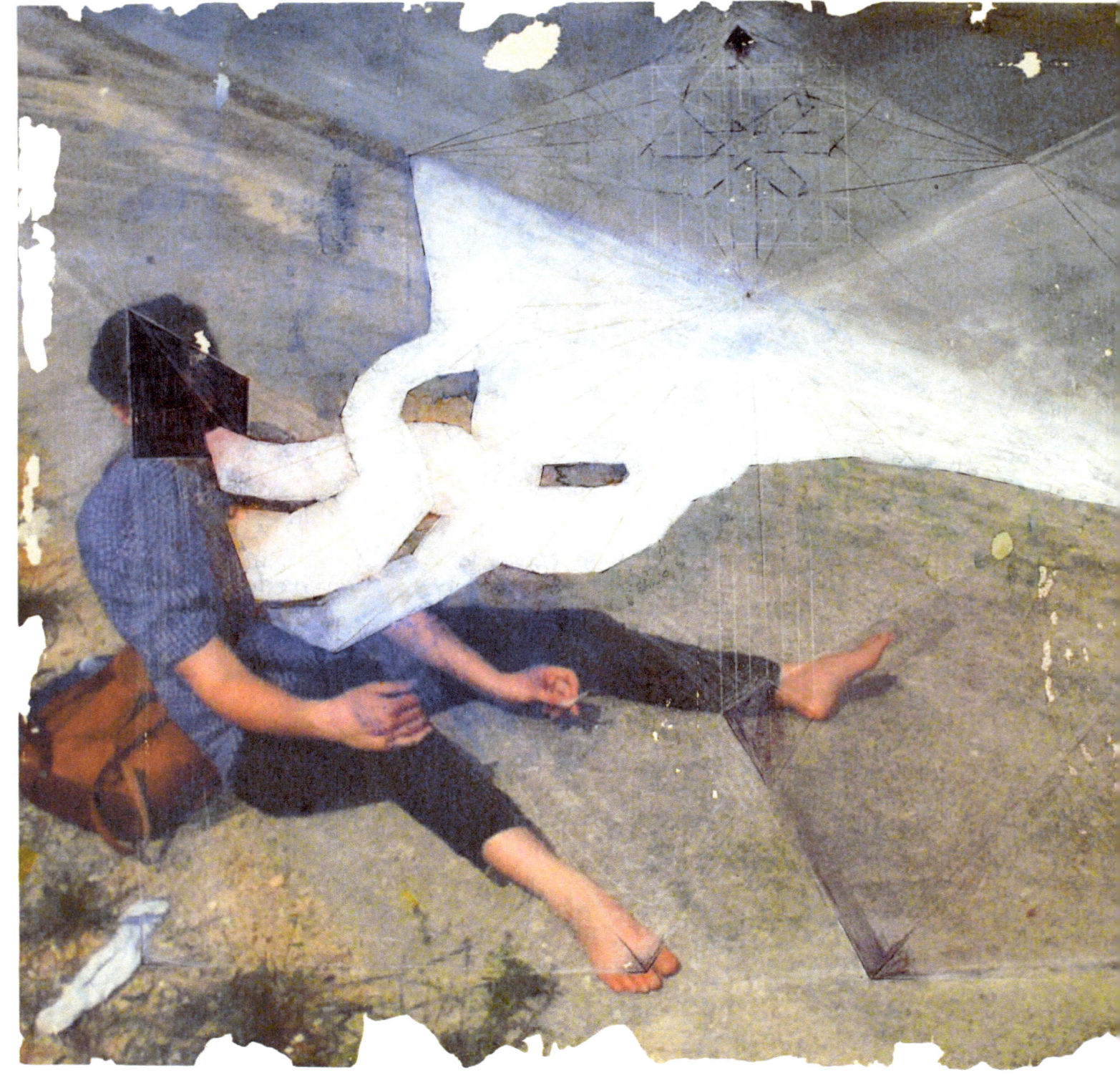

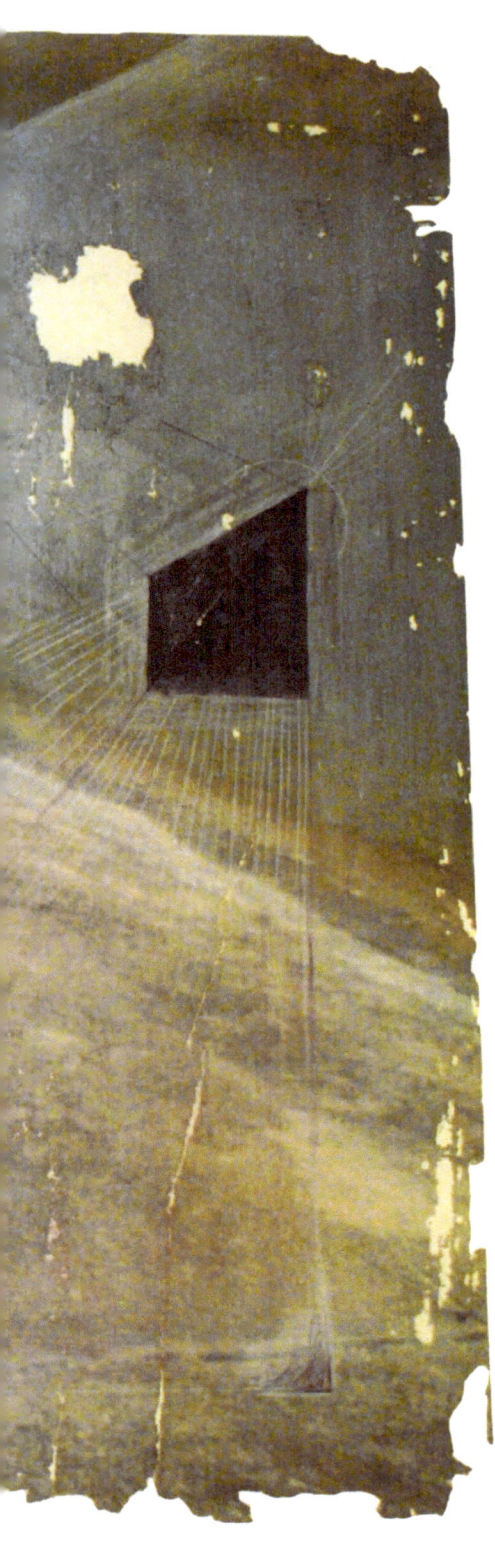

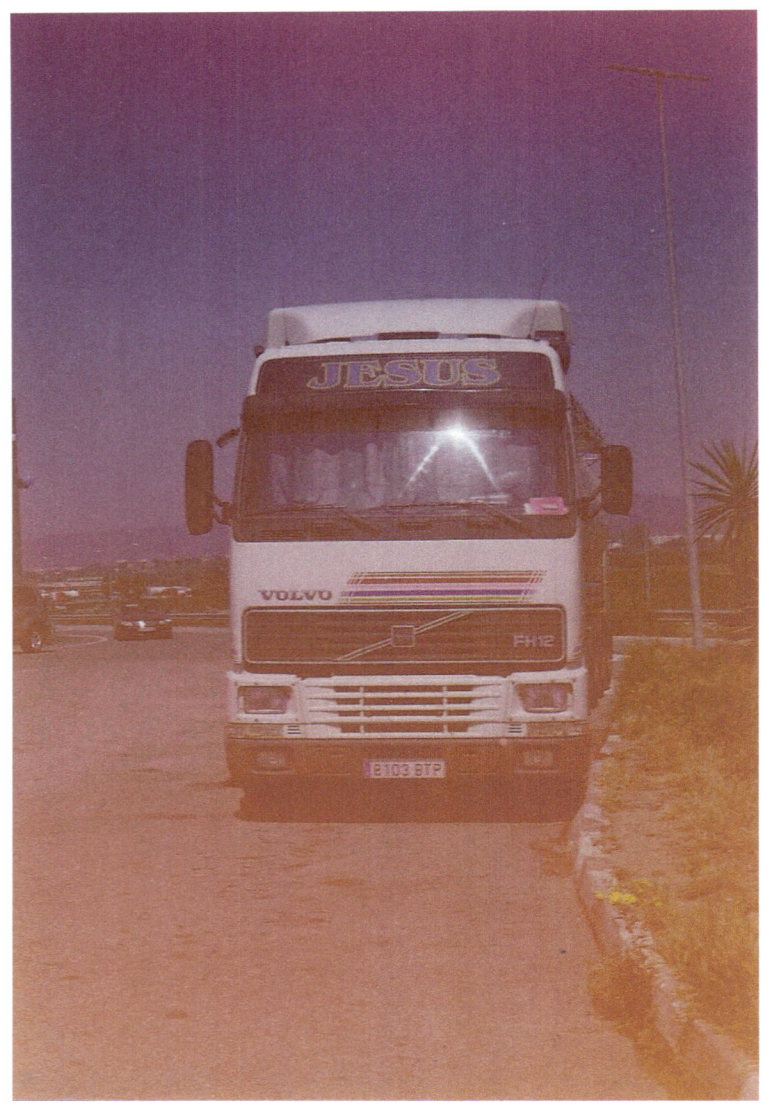

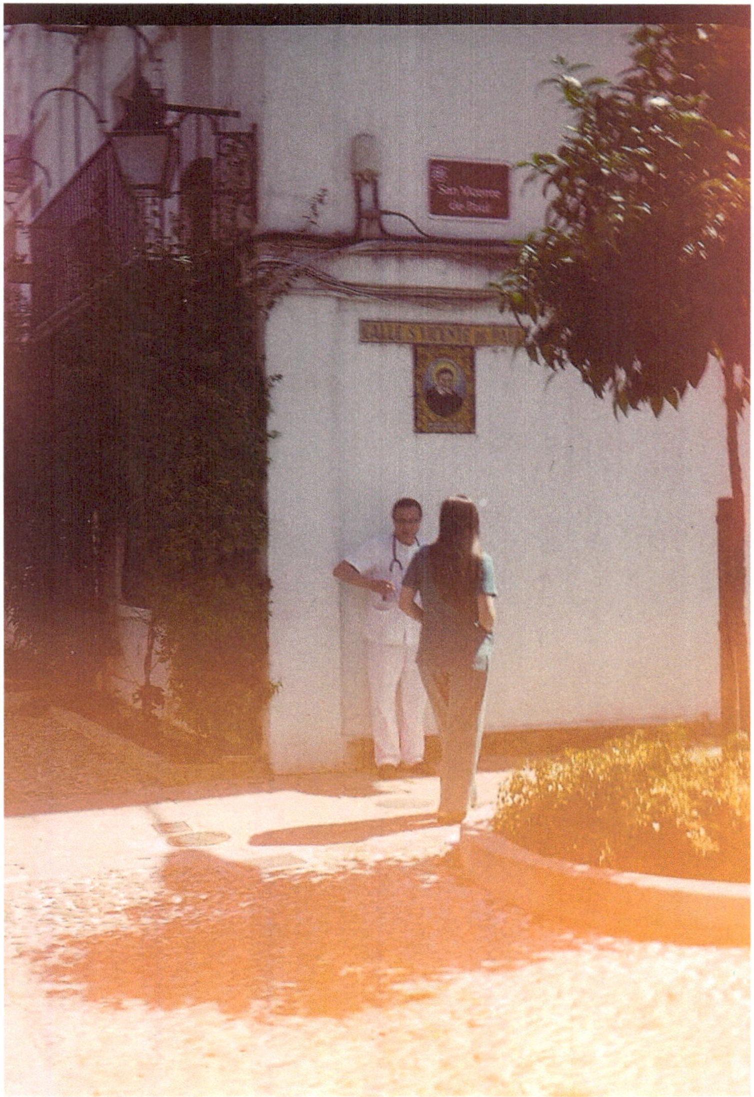

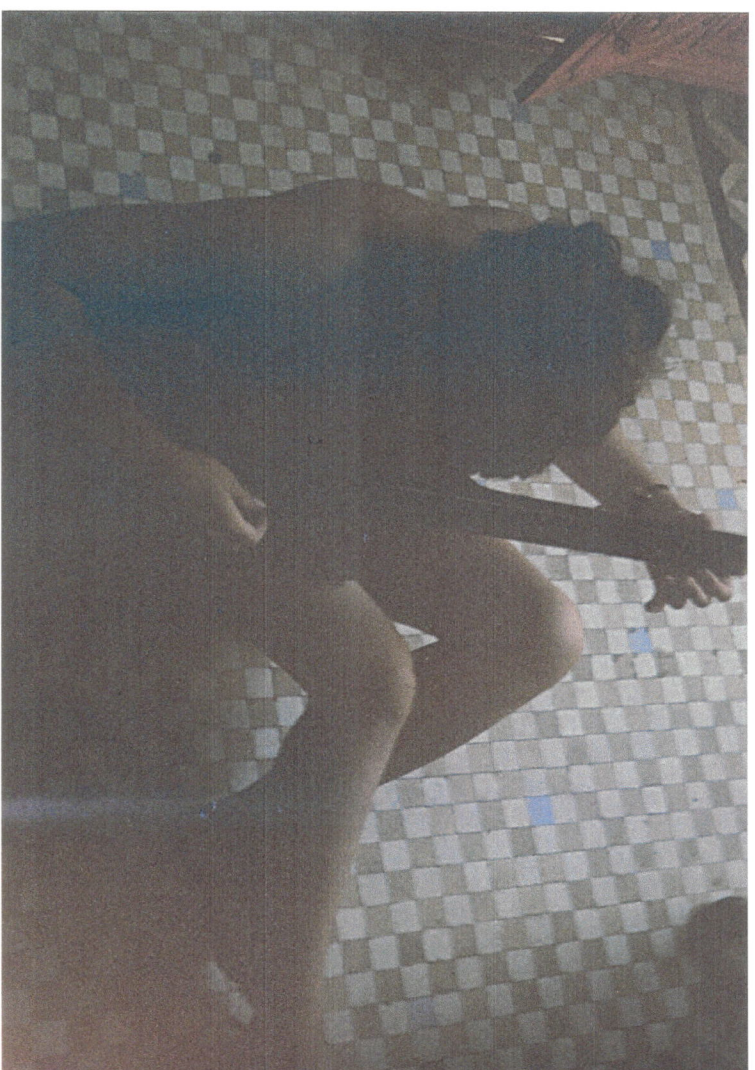

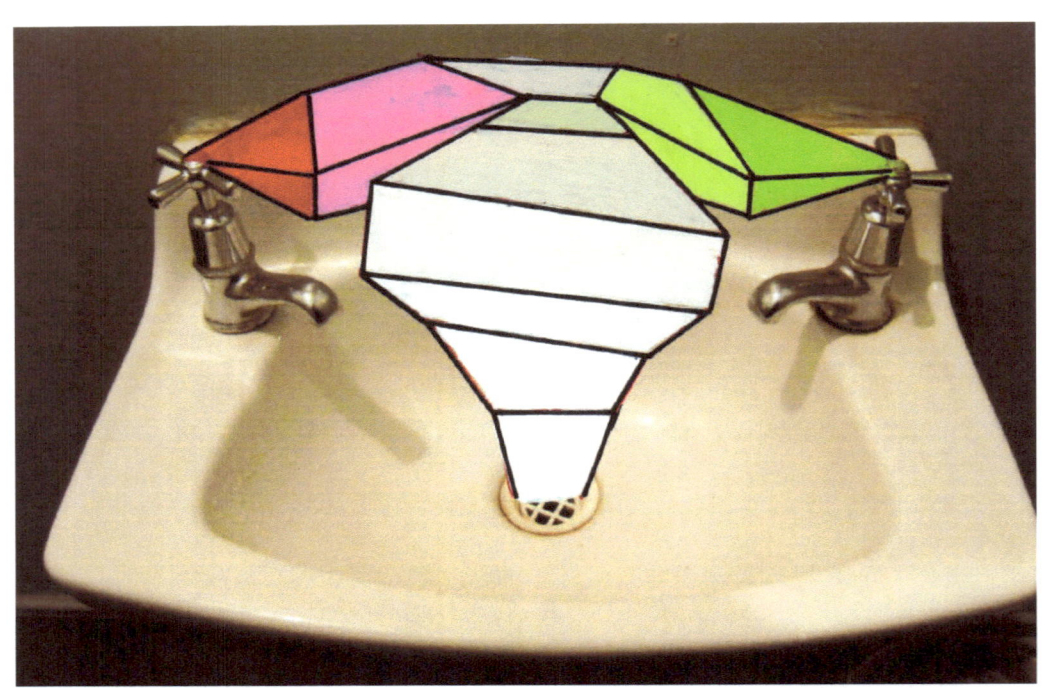
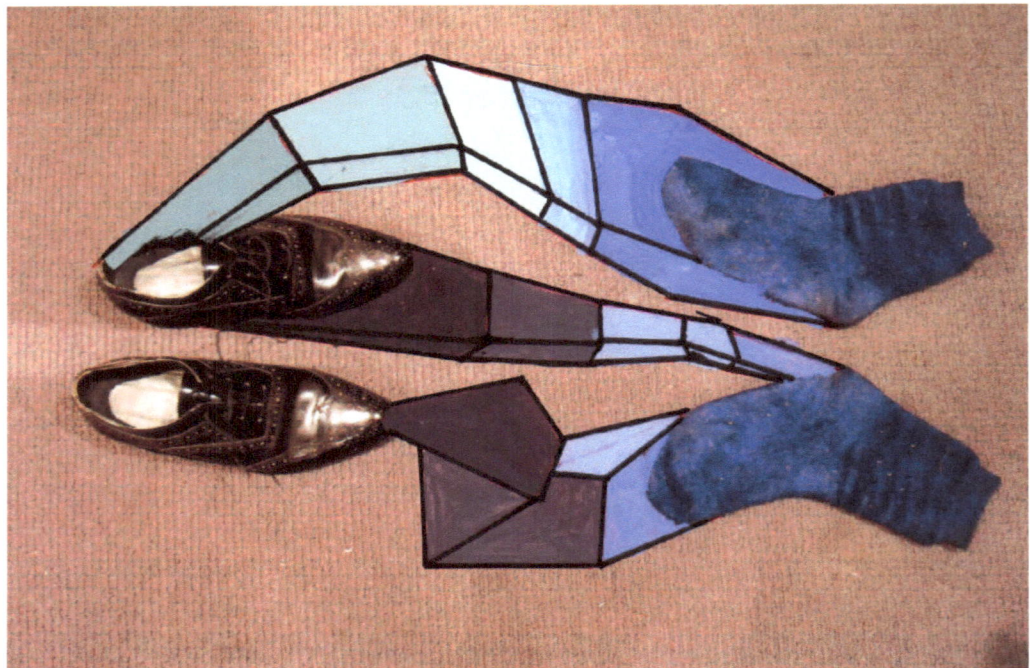

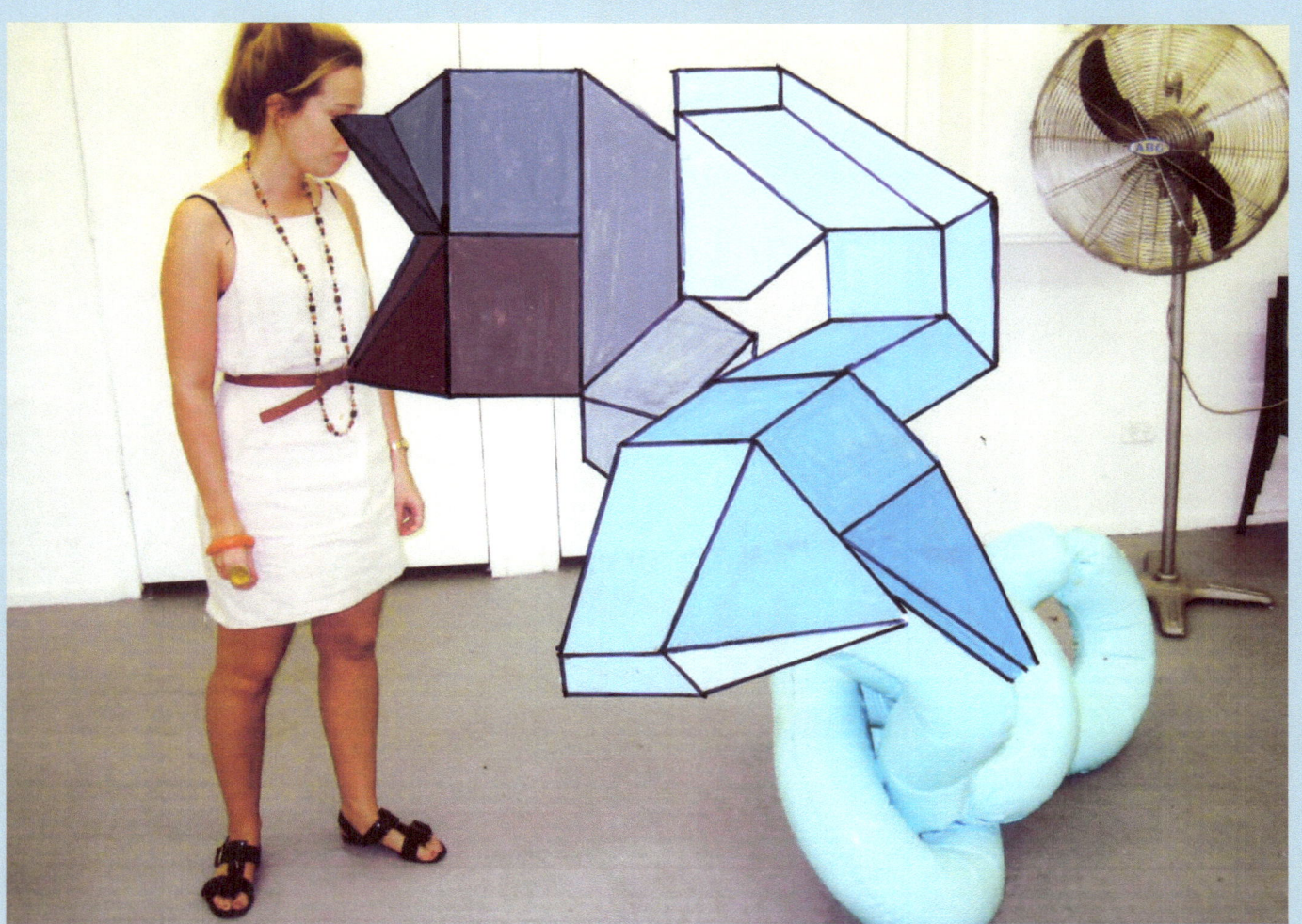

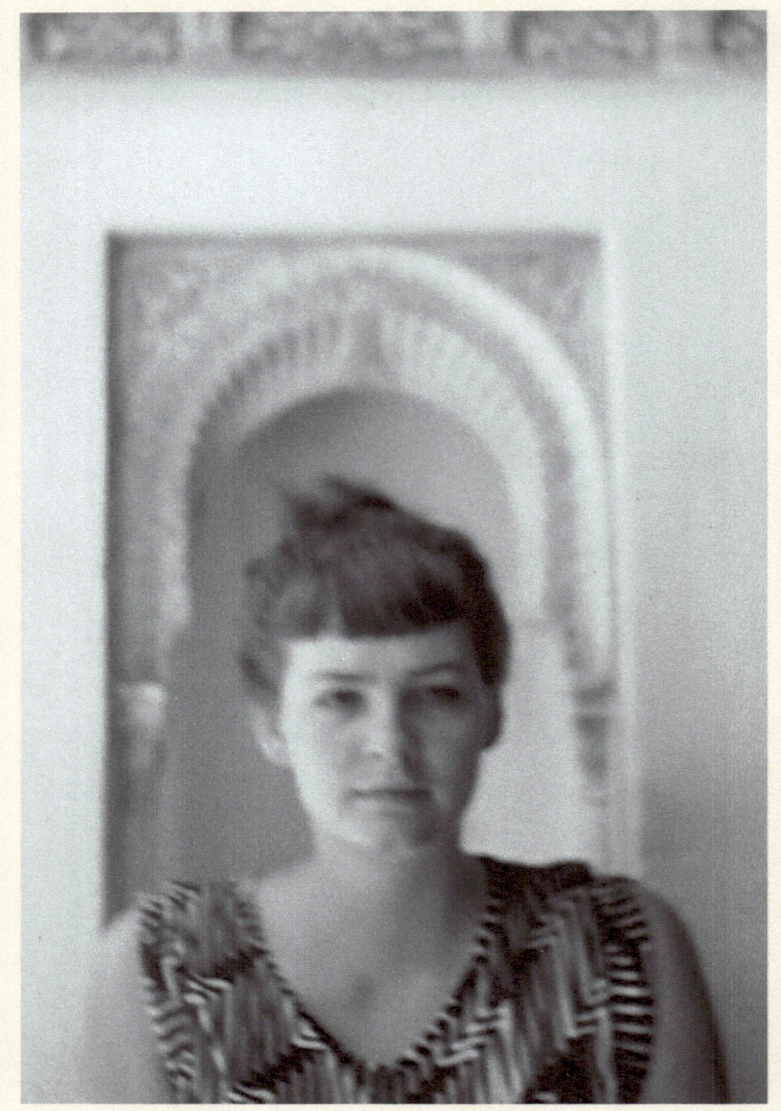

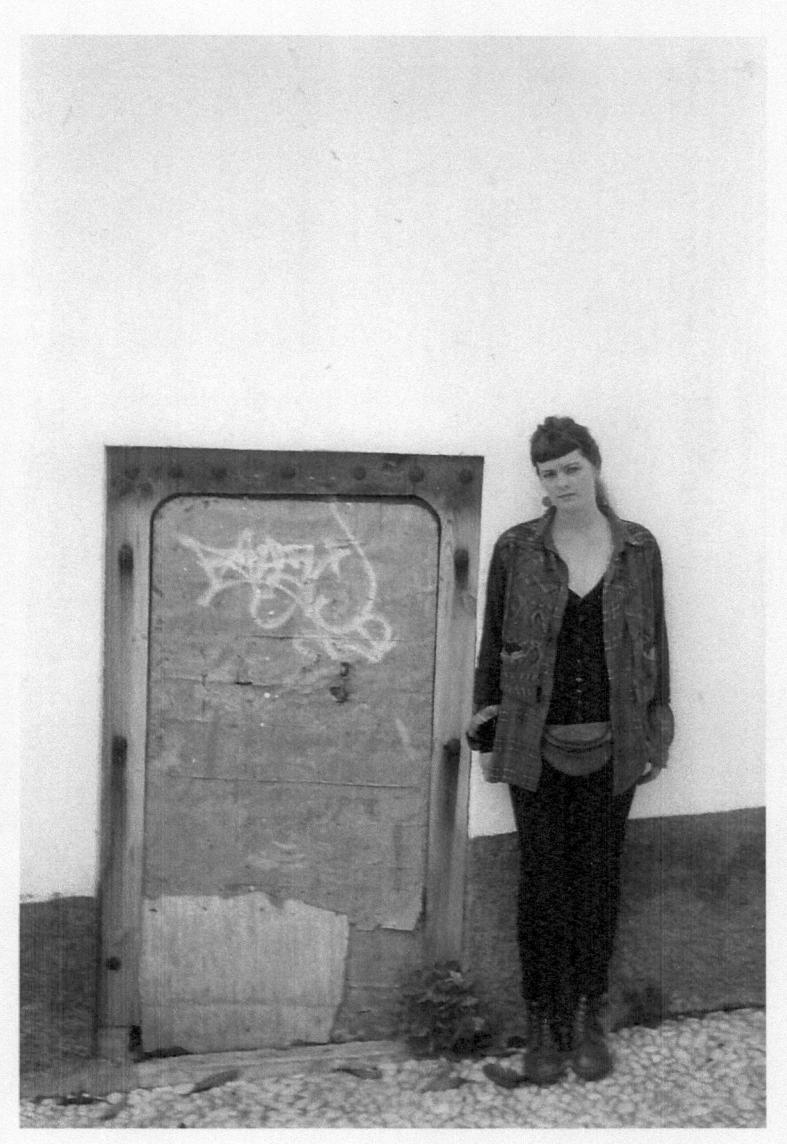

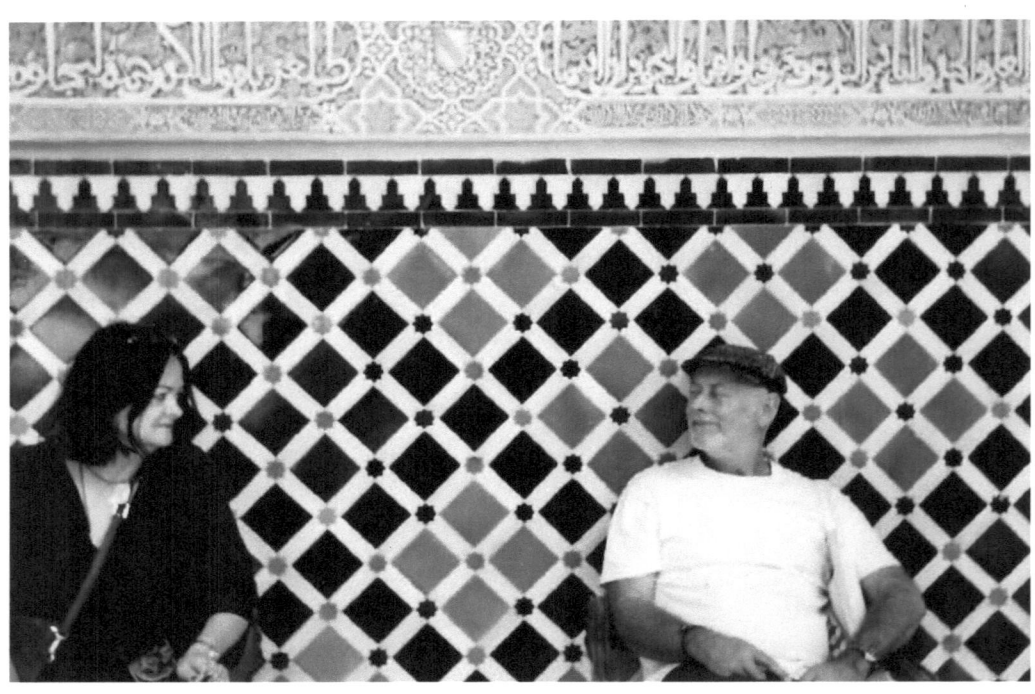